CONTENTS:

INTRODUCTION:

'The Merchant of Venice' is one of several of Shakespeare's plays which take place in a foreign setting. Just like 'Romeo and Juliet', this is a story which Shakespeare himself did not create. The 14th Century writer Giovanni Fiorentino wrote 'Il Pecorone' years before Shakespeare was born. 'Il Pecorone' tells the story of an upstanding young gentleman who travels to Belmont where he meets a rich widow. In order to woo her, he borrows money from a Jewish moneylender, which is ultimately paid for with a pound of flesh. It seems clear that one explanation for the Venetian setting is that the story originated there. Just as with 'Romeo and Juliet', the setting ties neatly into the plot. In Elizabethan England, Venice was a key trading centre. Exotic goods were traded in the city, which was home to the explorer Marco Polo. Venice is therefore a great setting for a story where trading is an intrinsic part of the plot.

It is also possible that Shakespeare set the play in Venice in order to distance himself slightly from the criticism of England which we find within the plot. 'The Merchant of Venice' contains several themes, one of which is the treatment of Jewish people. In Shakespeare's time, Jews had been banished from England. One interpretation is that Shakespeare uses the play to highlight the unjust treatment of the Jews. When Shylock asks "if you prick us do we not bleed?" it is easy to hear the voice of Shakespeare challenging his audience to face the fact that Jewish people are no different to them.

Another key theme of 'The Merchant of Venice' is the role of parent and child. Even after his death, Portia's father exerts control over how she will meet her future husband. When Portia asks Nerissa "Isn't it a pain that I can't choose or refuse anyone?", it is once again easy to hear the echo of Shakespeare's own challenge to the audience that we find in 'Romeo and Juliet'.

Analysis of Act 1

SCENE 1

'The Merchant of Venice' is a complex play. It contains a vast number of characters and numerous plot-lines. Therefore, it is essential that Shakespeare uses the opening scene to establish the main characters and storyline. In terms of structural analysis, this scene is one of several expositions found in the opening act.

Structure refers to the organisation of a text. The Greek philosopher Aristotle, around the year 335 BC, wrote 'Poetics', a book which included theories on narrative structure. Aristotle believed that drama could be divided into three sections. In the 19th Century, building on the work of Aristotle, the German novelist Gustav Freytag proposed that all five act plays follow the same format:

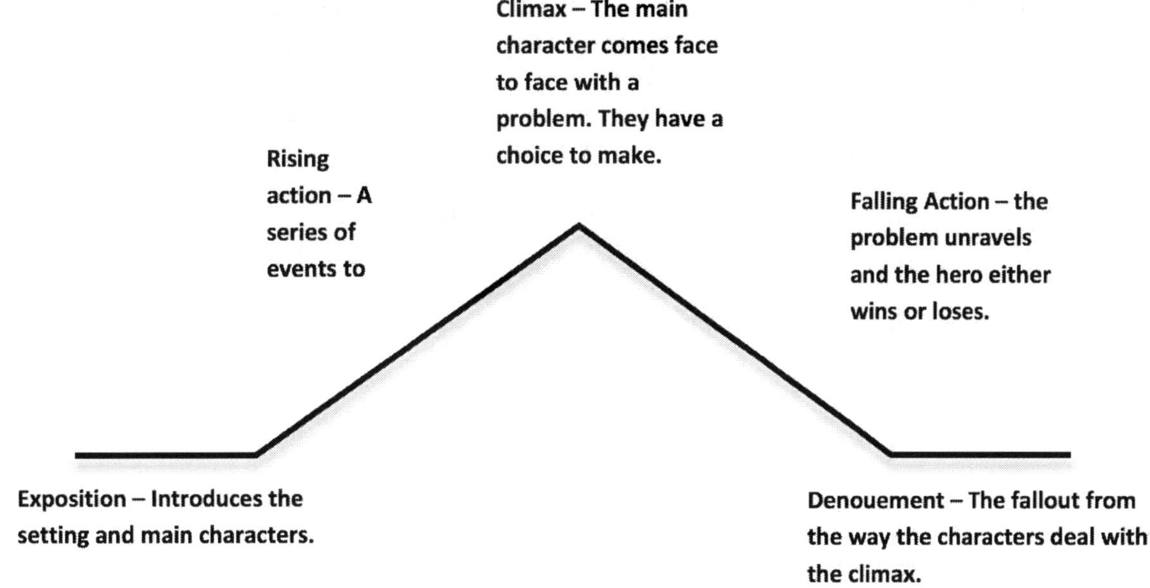
Climax – The main character comes face to face with a problem. They have a choice to make.
Rising action – A series of events to
Falling Action – the problem unravels and the hero either wins or loses.
Exposition – Introduces the setting and main characters.
Denouement – The fallout from the way the characters deal with the climax.

Following Freytag's pyramid, we learn many important points in this opening exposition scene:

1. Antonio is a successful merchant whose wealth is totally invested in trading- ships which are currently all at sea.

2. His friend, Bassanio, is in love with a rich lady called Portia. Bassanio wants to marry Portia, but first wishes to borrow money to make his lifestyle appropriately lavish in order to impress such a rich lady.

3. Antonio wants to lend Bassanio the money, but has none available as it is all invested in his trading- ships. He tells Bassanio that he can borrow money and use Antonio as a guarantor for the debt.

It is a sign of Shakespeare's talent that these details are revealed, not by Antonio, but by other characters. Knowing that Antonio, his friend, is depressed, Salarino wonders if it is due to the fact that "your mind is tossing on the ocean...where your argosies...overpeer the petty traffickers". What does this mean? Salarino is trying to encourage his friend Antonio that his huge merchant ships are far superior to other sea vessels. It is through the words of his friends that we discover a vital plot point: Antonio is currently risking his entire wealth on his trading- ships. If he loses his ships, he will lose all of his wealth.

The literary device of foreshadowing is used when Salarino mentions the 'dangerous rocks' which can wreck ships. Straight away, in this opening scene, Shakespeare lays out Antonio's situation and hints at how it will end. Cleverly, he does this not through the words of Antonio himself, but through those of Salarino and Solanio.

When Antonio enters the scene, the second piece of the exposition is revealed: the primary love story. Antonio asks Bassanio for an update on the 'pilgrimage' he wishes to embark upon. The word 'pilgrimage' is a religious word, referring to a religious journey to a sacred destination. This language suggests that Bassanio is truly in love, but Bassanio's reply suggests something different:

> *'My chief care*
>
> *Is to come fairly off from the great debts*
>
> *Wherein my time something too prodigal*
>
> *Hath left me gaged. To you, Antonio,*
>
> *I owe the most, in money and in love,*
>
> *And from your love I have a warranty*
>
> *To unburden all my plots and purposes*
>
> *How to get clear of all the debts I owe.'*

It appears that Bassanio wishes to marry Portia simply to inherit her wealth and to pay off his debts. Indeed, when asked to describe Portia, the structure of his reply is equally startling:

> *'In Belmont is a lady richly left;*
>
> *And she is fair, and, fairer than that word,*
>
> *Of wondrous virtues: sometimes from her eyes*
>
> *I did receive fair speechless messages:*
>
> *Her name is Portia, nothing undervalued*
>
> *To Cato's daughter, Brutus' Portia:*
>
> *Nor is the wide world ignorant of her worth,*
>
> *For the four winds blow in from every coast*
>
> *Renowned suitors, and her sunny locks*
>
> *Hang on her temples like a golden fleece;*
>
> *Which makes her seat of Belmont Colchos' strand,*

And many Jasons come in quest of her.

O my Antonio, had I but the means

To hold a rival place with one of them,

I have a mind presages me such thrift,

That I should questionless be fortunate!'

Despite supposedly being in love with Portia, the very first thing Bassanio chooses to mention is her wealth. After appraising her wealth, Bassanio moves on to a description of her physical appearance – 'she is fair', 'sunny locks'. This also does not paint a positive picture of Bassanio, who seems only to be interested in money and sex. We learn nothing of Portia's personality in this speech. Even the references to her looks are intertextual references to wealth. The 'golden fleece' simile is a reference to the Greek myth of Jason and the Argonuats. In this tale, Jason wanted to take his place as king. In order to do so, he had to find a magical ram and take its golden fleece. The reference portrays Portia as the golden fleece, and Bassanio on a journey to claim her. When he is married to Portia, Bassanio will be, like Jason, king of his domain. This reference clearly portrays women as objects to be possessed. It's not a great start for Bassanio.

ACT 1 SCENE 2

Having established the Antonio / Bassanio storyline, Shakespeare now moves on to another set of characters – that of Portia and Nerissa. This alternating structure is found throughout the text, often at moments of great tension. It is one of Shakespeare's structural devices which is employed to keep the audience engaged and to heighten the tension in the play. Just as something important is revealed, such as when we learn that Bassanio is going to try to borrow money and have Antonio as his guarantor, the focus of the drama moves to a different set of characters.

From the description of her in Act 1 Scene 1, we might be forgiven for thinking that Portia will be a weak and insipid character. How wrong that assumption would be!

Act 1 Scene 2 opens with Portia's line:

'By my troth, Nerissa, my little body is aweary of this great world'.

This line echoes Antonio's opening of the previous scene, where he proclaimed:

'In sooth, I know not why I am so sad'.

Shakespeare deliberately juxtaposes the sadness of Antonio with the sadness of Portia in the opening lines of the first two scenes. However, Portia's sadness is clearly much more justified than that of ambiguous Antonio. Portia reveals that she has no choice over the man she is set to marry. Her deceased father has arranged the terms of the marriage. Portia expresses her frustration to her maid, Nerissa:

'I may neither choose who I would nor refuse who I dislike; so is the will of a living daughter curb'd by the will of a dead father'.

Whilst a modern audience would most probably be shocked by this, an Elizabethan audience would perhaps not find this a shocking prospect.

In Shakespeare's time the legal age for a female to get married was just twelve years old, although most women got married in their twenties, similar to today. In 2013 the average UK age of marriage is 28 for a woman, whereas in 1590 it was 27. However, a special exception was sometimes made for rich and noble families, who would often marry off their young children for reasons of property and family alliance. If your family had money and my family had land, our parents may want us to marry so that, through linking the families by our marriage, they have both money and land. Because Portia undoubtedly comes from a rich family, an Elizabethan audience would expect her to be the subject of an arranged marriage.

Portia is clearly unhappy about her father's decree and so we might wonder why she does not ignore it. It is important to understand the historical context here. In Shakespeare's time, women were seen as little more than mothers and objects of male desire. Most women were denied anything beyond a basic education. Even when girls did go to grammar schools, many classes had 'male only' signs on the doors; girls would only be taught the most basic subjects. Upper class families like Portia's would hire tutors to teach their children, but even then, the prospects for an educated woman were very limited. Women could not enter any profession nor even vote, but instead were prepared for domestic lives. Upper class girls were taught how to cook, sew, play instruments and become proficient in other activities which might be considered to make domestic life more attractive.

The only option for a woman was to get married and to run the household. With this in mind, we can see that Portia, (and all women of the time), was fated to get married. Today women have no need to marry, but failure to find a husband in Shakespeare's time meant a desperate life.

Females could only survive through the men who provided for them. As children, girls would rely on their fathers for financial support and protection. When they married, this responsibility passed onto the husband. It was almost unheard of not to marry; if a woman didn't wed there were only two other options available: to become a nun or to become a prostitute. This shocking contextual detail helps us to see the situation Portia is in.

Given the great contextual pressures Portia finds herself subject to, it is perhaps a great surprise to see that she is so witty. Act 1 Scene 2 is filled with word-play and humour from Portia. When commenting on the Neapolitan prince who talked of nothing but his horse, she jokes with Nerissa that:

> *'I am much afear'd my lady, his mother, play'd false with a smith'.*

The joke being made here is that the prince talked so much about horses that he was probably the son of a blacksmith – an iron worker whose job included shoeing horses.

Portia also proclaims:

> *'I had rather be married to a death's-head with a bone in his mouth than to either of these'.*

These words echo those of Beatrice in the opening scene of 'Much Ado About Nothing':

> *'I had rather hear my dog bark at a crow than a man swear he loves me'.*

Portia, presented here to the audience as a powerful woman skilled in verbal combat, foreshadows the later scenes where she will go into verbal battle with Shylock. Shakespeare often presents women as his strongest characters.

It is clear that Portia is intelligent, head-strong and witty. This makes it all the more sad that she is not allowed to choose her own husband but must be 'obtained by the manner of my father's will'. However, the scene ends with a glimpse of positivity.

The Merchant of Venice is a comedy and therefore it is important that Shakespeare points the way to the happy ending. This is indicated when Portia and Nerissa talk about Bassanio, referred to by Portia as 'worthy of thy praise'. Despite the negativity contained in the opening two scenes, this moment hints to the audience that there will, as is required in a comedy, be a happy ending to look forward to.

GENRE: COMEDY

The genre of comedy does not mean that the play will be filled with jokes and humour. There will be witty word-play and puns, but comedies often contain dark and sinister moments too.

The easiest way to identify a comedy is to compare it to other genres. Whereas a tragedy ends in death, a comedy often ends in marriage. Comedies also contain complex plots and cases of mistaken identity. These conventions are found in most of the 18 Shakespeare plays which are identified as comedies. However, they are all found in The Merchant of Venice and because of this, a knowledgeable audience would know that the play is going to end positively, with Portia and

Bassanio getting married. Despite the negativity of the opening two scenes, an audience would not be concerned; they would simply be keen to see how the relationship will play out.

ACT 1 SCENE 3

In this final scene of the opening act, the audience is introduced to the character of Shylock. Shakespeare's stage directions indicate that Shylock is a Jew. In Elizabethan England, there were no Jewish people as they had been exiled from the country many years before. With this in mind, we need to appreciate the fact that Jews had an almost mythical image in Shakespeare's world. Today we read this play as racist and uncomfortable, but in Elizabethan England there would have been a sense of detachment from Shylock the Jew.
Bassanio is presented as desperate in this scene. He asks Shylock a triple question:

'May you stead me? Will you pleasure me? Shall I know your answer?'

By asking three questions in a row, Bassanio does not leave any time for Shylock to answer. This is one of many examples where we see Bassanio as an impatient and immature character.

Next we see an example from Shylock of foreshadowing. Foreshadowing, as mentioned earlier, is a literary device where a writer hints at something that is going to happen later in the text. Foreshadowing is used extensively in this play. It could be argued that it is over-used, in fact. There is overkill, as there is in much of Shakespeare's writing.

In this example we see Shylock talk about 'The peril of waters, winds and rocks', foreshadowing the fact that Antonio's merchandise will ultimately be lost, and therefore his fortune lost at sea in a storm. We have to consider why Shakespeare is constantly foreshadowing what is to come. It could be because the audience is comprised of people with different levels of intellect and he needs to make the play accessible and enjoyable for everybody. There is very clever word-play at times, but at other times it is blatantly obvious what is going to happen. Perhaps he does this to bridge the gap between the intellectual and the not-so-intellectual in the audience. However, as we analyse the play, it can be a little annoying as the literary device of foreshadowing features so frequently.

Shylock's character is established in interesting ways in this scene. To begin with, he is shown to be a villain. In an aside Shylock says, among other things:

> *'I hate him for he is a Christian'.*

An aside is a quiet declaration to the audience. Shakespeare uses asides solely with heroes and villains. He uses asides to make it obvious whether the character is a good guy, or a bad guy and to make intentions instantly clear to audiences. What we can establish from this aside is that Shylock is a 'bad-guy'. He is presented from the outset as an archetypal villain who is going to pursue the downfall of Bassanio and Antonio.

There are also many biblical references in this play. Shylock says:

> *'You neither lend nor borrow upon advantage'*

He's talking to Antonio who is a Christian, challenging and reminding him that the bible states that you shouldn't loan for profit or borrow money.

That reflects the words of Jesus. The belief at this time was that Christians shouldn't be involved in money-lending, because Jesus taught that we shouldn't lend money for profit and shouldn't borrow money and get into debt. Jews don't adhere to the teachings of Jesus, as they don't believe that Jesus is the Messiah but rather believe that the Messiah is yet to come. So money lending became a Jewish occupation because it didn't conflict with their religious beliefs. That is why Shylock throws the bible back at Antonio, saying in effect that he shouldn't be involved in the money lending business at all.

Antonio is criticised here. The situation is, of course, that Christians will lend money, but not for profit. That fact makes Christians a business threat to Jewish money lenders. Shylock talks about times where he lost business because Antonio lent money and charged no interest. The situation is that Antonio is willing to lend money; he was going to lend Bassanio money but he didn't have any available, as all of his finances were tied up in his trading-ships. It is also established in Act1 Scene 1 that Antonio has lent Bassanio money previously. However, Antonio refuses to compromise his beliefs by lending money for profit and therefore he doesn't charge interest on his loans.

Shylock is therefore angry with Antonio because he is a business threat to him. Shylock makes a living out of lending money for profit. We can see the historical feud and where it originates.

At this point the audience's views of Shylock are starting to become conflicted. They can understand Shylock's attitude. He is trying to make a living and the way Antonio operates, regarding lending money, although helpful to others, is detrimental to Shylock's business.

You could think that Shylock is a complete villain, but then this perception is challenged when he says:

> *'You call me misbeliever, cut-throat dog, and spit upon my Jewish gaberdine'.*

This is where we see the first emergence of racism. It actually challenges the audience's opinion of Shylock who has been presented up until this point as a villain. We begin to consider the possibility that he could be a victim because he is being spat upon.

One of Shakespeare's great skills in this play is to toy with the audience over how they should feel about the character of Shylock. He can be viewed as either a victim or a villain. There's a constant fluctuation between the two. In your exams and assessments you should explain both sides of the argument, and demonstrate how the interpretation is not simple and straight forward.

Shylock subsequently introduces the wager. He says that he will lend Bassanio the money but if he can't pay it back on time, then Shylock will be entitled to cut off a pound of Antonio's flesh. He follows this offer up with the phrase:

> *'I extend this friendship'.*

Shylock is pretending that this is an innocuous game, setting up a silly bet where the forfeit is a pound of flesh, if the debt is not paid. He presents this offer as if it is a joke and in no way likely to be enforced.

The audience is conflicted because we know that, even in this scene, we have seen suggestions that Shylock is the villain, but also suggestions that Shylock is a victim. So, perhaps, we might think that this is his chance for him to redeem himself.

Shakespeare has cleverly used this scene and the interlacing of the two different views of the character Shylock, to make us unsure of how we should perceive him. We just don't know at this point in the play. Antonio agrees to the terms of the loan.

Antonio's response is:

> *'In this there can be no dismay, my ships come home a month before the day'.*

This is a presentation of Antonio as naïve because it seems to us, the audience, blatantly obvious that this is going to go horribly wrong. We wonder why Antonio can't anticipate the seemingly inevitable. It seems to us in Act 1, Scene 1 that Bassanio is presented as a bit of a fool who falls in love easily and frequently but Antonio doesn't seem to see it. I think we are led to believe that Antonio, although he is a wildly successful and rich merchant, can be rather naïve.

STRUCTURE OF THE PLAY – FREYTAG'S PYRAMID

It was the Greek philosopher Aristotle who in around 300 BC came up with the first ideas about how plays are structured.
In the 1800's Gustav Freytag said that all five act plays followed this structure:

1. There is an exposition which introduces the setting and main characters
2. Rising action – a series of events to keep the audience interested,
3. The climax – the big main event of the whole story
4. The falling action
5. The Dénouement

In Act 1, Scene 3, the exposition is now complete. The money is lent, all the characters have been established, and all the main storylines are in place, although there are some sub-plots yet to develop. We see the opposition of the characters of Antonio and Shylock. Antonio is presented as trusting and naïve and Shylock as cunning and sly. In the presentations of these two characters we can see plenty of potential for conflict in the play.

Shakespeare uses the structural device of having only 3 scenes in Act 1 instead of the customary 5. He has established everything needed for the exposition and moves quickly on, wasting no time, to Act 2. It is time for the rising action.

Analysis of Act 2

Act 2, Scene 1

Act Two, Scene one is a very short scene. Shakespeare often varied the lengths of his scenes and when you are reading this play it is important to think about how that would look on stage. Remember that Shakespeare was writing for the stage and that he wasn't writing with the expectation of people reading his works, apart, that is, from his actors, in order to learn their lines.

This scene, if you were watching it on stage, would probably last about two minutes. That may sound ridiculous but in Shakespeare's day there was no scenery change. There were no sets, or backgrounds to swap. The actors would just come out and act the scene.

There are two things to remember. The first is that the actors would come out on stage and there would be no background scenery or props. The second thing to remember is that in Shakespeare's time all of the actors were male! You may wonder how that works. How do you have, in this scene, Portia and Morocco? It is in fact a man who plays the role of Portia. This play already features female characters dressing as men, so when you think of the scenes where Portia disguises herself as a man, you realise that it would be a man, dressing up as a woman, who dresses up as a man again! They would often choose young, feminine men to play the women, perhaps young men whose voices hadn't yet broken.

It is important to think about how the play would have come across on stage in Shakespeare's time, compared to how it would appear in modern times. These plays are still enacted today, and nowadays women play the female roles, and of course there are now props, scenery and backdrops freely available.

This whole scene would be over very quickly, as would the next one. If you actually map out all of the scenes in the play, it is interesting to think about how they change in terms of pace and tempo. Sometimes short scenes are comic interludes, and we see that in Act 2, Scene 2.

Act 2 scene 1, however, covers a very serious topic. We are introduced to the prince of Morocco who is a black man. We have already considered the fact that Jews did not live in England in Shakespeare's time, so we have to think about who would have played the role of Shylock and how they would have enacted a Jew. Similarly, we wonder whether characters from different countries would have been played by white men and whether they would have had to speak with a foreign accent.

There is a prevalent theme of racism throughout the play and it is evident in this scene as the prince of Morocco begins by saying :

> *'Mislike me not for my complexion, the shadowed livery of a burnished sun, to whom I am a neighbour, near-bred'.*

In more contemporary language this would read :

> *'I'm dark skinned, please don't dislike me because of that'*

It is interesting that these are the first words that Morocco says. He clearly anticipates and argues against what he thinks will be Portia's response, before she even has a chance to say it. It hints at the fact that racism is embedded in this society. So this is one of many moments, similar to the ones with Shylock, where we, as a modern audience, would have a different reaction to an Elizabethan audience. Some of these scenes seem quite uncomfortable to us because they focus on the colour of skin and intolerance of differing religious beliefs.

Portia's response is interesting. She says:

> *'Yourself, renowned prince, then stood as fair as any comer I have look'd on yet for my affection'*

This is one of many times where Portia's words have a double meaning. She is telling the prince of Morocco that she doesn't look down on him because he is black, but that he has as good a chance as anyone else she has seen.

This is an example of dramatic irony where the audience know something that the characters on stage don't, in this case Morocco. Morocco doesn't know, but we, the audience do know, that Portia doesn't like any of her suitors yet! So Portia's words have double meaning, a bit of wordplay. The prince of Morocco will probably interpret her words that Portia thinks that he is as amazing as everyone else. In reality Portia is saying that she doesn't like Morocco or any of her suitors so far and so he isn't set apart from anybody.

He obviously takes it positively though, so we can consider whether Portia is trying to save his feelings.

Portia is very polite in male company, which hints at the climate of male dominance in Elizabethan society. When she is with Nerissa in the previous scene, there is a lot of joking and banter. Here though, when there are men present, Portia is more subservient, respectful and polite. This hints at the situation in Elizabethan England where there was inequality between men and women. Even though she doesn't like this man, she doesn't like the prospect of marrying him, and she doesn't like the situation she's been put in, she is still polite and cordial to him. However, she consistently maintains that witty banter, and extremely clever approach to language which we begin to sense will become important when she eventually goes into verbal battle with Shylock.

Bassanio appears to be a moping fool! Antonio appears to be a depressed guy who doesn't make good decisions. Shylock is clever, cunning, sophisticated and sly. We could easily wonder however this play is going to have a happy ending.

However, Shakespeare is already sowing the seeds to suggest that Portia is going to bring about the happy ending, that she's going to save the day. This reflects Shakespeare's positivity about women.

Portia explains to each of her suitors:

'If you choose wrong you have to swear never to speak to lady again in way of marriage'

It is revealed that part of the ruling is that if the suitors choose the wrong casket, they cannot marry another woman. It is interesting that none of the suitors argue with this stipulation. However, the reality is, that in this male dominated society where women have no power, the men could just go away and do whatever they liked. The men had much more freedom, sexually, than women, who were restricted. In those days women had to remain pure and marriage was the only option for them, whereas men would be off gallivanting and the way they lived was regarded as acceptable.

Act 2, Scene 1 is a very short scene which gives us an insight into Portia's character and sets the tension building for her verbal battle with Shylock later on in the play.

ACT 2 SCENE 2

This is a light hearted, comic scene. Humorous scenes are often used to contrast the seriousness of the previous scene. In the previous scene Portia talks to the prince of Morocco. Even though Portia uses some clever wordplay to entertain the audience, it is quite a sad scene. She might be about to marry someone she doesn't want to marry, having been forced into the situation.

So it's time to lighten the mood with an equally short scene, but one with a completely different vibe. This one is a comical scene. This scene introduces us to Launcelot and Old Gobbo. You will observe that Launcelot's and Old Gobbo's words are in prose. Prose is often utilised for characters of lesser intelligence, which gives us insight into the skill of Shakespeare's writing.

Launcelot is Shylock's servant, and he wants to go to work for Bassanio. It's a very amusing scene. We mustn't mistake the genre of comedy in Shakespeare's time with modern day comedy. In Shakespeare's time the genre of comedy was demonstrated by plays in which the characters didn't die at the end of the story but, rather, they ended with happy marriages. Shakespearean comedies also contained scenes of mistaken identity. Modern day comedies are identified by having overtly humorous storylines.

There are, however, funny moments in this scene. The conversation between Launcelot and his father, Old Gobbo, is deliberately humorous. Launcelot says that Old Gobbo's son is dead. He's trying to trick Old Gobbo into thinking his son has died, even though Launcelot is his son. It's entertaining because the father doesn't even recognise his own son telling him this. He says:

> *'Ergo master Launcelot. Talk not of master Launcelot. Father for the young gentleman, according to the fates and destinies and such old sayings, the sisters three and such branches of learning, is indeed deceased'*

In short, Launceolot is telling Old Gobbo that his son is dead.

Now Old Gobbo is really upset and says:

> *'Marry, God forbid! The boy was the very staff of my age, my very prop'*

They have this humorous banter back and forth, where Launcelot is in effect asking Old Gobbo why, if his son meant so much to him, he can't recognise him stood in front of him!

There is, however, a deeper meaning to this line:

> *'...is indeed deceased'*

It is one of the many references to the theme of trickery and lies. There is so much deception in this play. This is just one light-hearted, humorous example of it but ultimately there is deception throughout the play.

Shakespeare once again makes use of the literary device of foreshadowing by saying:

> *'In the end truth will out'*

These words are spoken by Launcelot, but it's a hint at the fact that by the time we get to the end of the play the truth about everything will be revealed. Foreshadowing is something that Shakespeare does all the time, hinting at what is to come later. It can seem quite basic but there is the acceptance that there would be people in the audience intelligent enough to grasp all of the subtle comedy, and people who were less intelligent and would need to be helped through it.

Interestingly, Launcelot wants to work for Bassanio. Opinions about Bassanio are varied at this point. We know that Portia likes him, and I suppose that holds some weight because we respect Portia and have no reason to dislike her. We get the sense that she is intelligent and articulate. There is some racism in what she says, but contextually that would have been understood. So, if we respect Portia's character, then we can, perhaps, warm a little to Bassanio because Portia likes him: If Portia likes him, and Portia is a good person, then maybe we should like him too.

The difficulty with that is that everything we have seen of Bassanio so far, presents him as immature, flighty, unable to think things through, too heavily reliant on his friends, lacking in maturity and unable to look after things properly. So I still think that at this point the jury is out on Bassanio.

However, there is talk in this scene of Bassanio being a good person. Launcelot wants to quit working for Shylock and go to work for Bassanio. He says:

'I'm glad you have come, father. Give me your present to one master Bassanio who indeed gives rare new liveries. If I serve not him, I will run as far as God has any ground'

Launcelot is asking his father to help him to get a job with Bassanio who gives his servants particularly smart uniforms. He goes on to say that if he doesn't get a job with Bassanio, he will run away.

When Launcelot says he 'gives rare new liveries', he means that Bassanio provides his servants with expensive uniforms. However, this causes us concern because it shows us that Bassanio is frittering away the money which he has borrowed from his friend because he wants to make a good impression on Portia. Bassanio is being reckless with money.

Probably the funniest part of this scene is the conversation between Launcelot and Old Gobbo where there are a lot of malapropisms. This is an example of word play, where a word is incorrectly used but sounds like the one that should be used. However, when you use the incorrect word, it has a completely ridiculous meaning. Old Gobbo says:

> *'He hath a great infection, sir, as one would say to serve'*

He is asking Bassanio to take his son on as a servant.

But he's supposed to say:

> *'He hath a great **affection**, sir, as one would say to serve'*

He's trying to say his son is very keen to serve, but instead says his son has a great infection! Launcelot doesn't correct his father, suggesting that he isn't so clever either. In fact Launcelot gives an example of a malapropism himself. He says:

> *'To be brief, the very truth is that the Jew, having done me wrong, doth cause me, as my father, being I hope an old man shall fruitify unto you'*

In this case, fruitify is the wrong word. It's supposed to be '**certify**'. Old Gobbo goes on to say:

> *'That is the very **defect** of the matter, sir'*

But he should have said:

> *'That is the very **effect** of the matter sir'*

A malapropism is where a word is used that sounds like the correct word, but has a completely different meaning, resulting in a comic effect. It's something that Shakespeare is very good at, and he regularly gives these to his comic characters. In *Romeo and Juliet*, the nurse often speaks in this way. It's a cheap joke for the audience which would cause everyone to burst out laughing. It's not particularly clever word play, but rather, it's just a simple joke.

In this scene we have not just light hearted comedy, but the establishment of sub-plots. Gratiano says:

> *'You must not deny me. I must go with you to Belmont'*

We see here the beginning of one of the other love storylines, which is one of the conventions that is important in a comedy. Comedies tend to have several different, confusing love stories.

Launcelot then leaves Shylock. You could argue that this foreshadows Jessica doing the same in the next scene. Things are falling apart for Shylock, people around him are leaving. Losing Launcelot is just a small loss, but in the next scene losing his daughter, Jessica, is a huge loss.

In most other Acts, Scene 1 develops minor plot points such as Launcelot's change of employer, but here, we see it in Scene 2. We are provided with little bits of the plot which will become important to the storyline as it unfolds.

This Scene is slapstick and visual comedy. The dialogue is not witty as it was in Portia's scene. The action is witty instead. It's kind of lowest-common-denominator, basic, simplistic comedy. There's an expectation that the dialogue between Launcelot and Gobbo would be delivered with the two men stood in line. One would pop up and say his bit, then duck down and then the other would pop up and say his bit, then duck down. It's very Laurel and Hardy, Chuckle Brothers 'To me, to you' light hearted comedy. On the other hand, almost everything Portia says is witty, but you have to work it out. Shakespeare provides laughter for everybody, throughout all of his plays. (At least, the ones which are supposed to be, in some way, comical!)

Act Two, Scenes Three, Four, Five and Six

Act 2, Scene 3, and the following scenes are very short scenes. In Elizabethan England this wouldn't have been an issue because there was no scenery to change, no backdrop or props to bring on. However, for modern theatre these scenes pose a number of problems because they are so quick. This first one has just twenty-one lines!

These are important scenes though. They quickly reveal lots of information about what's going on. One of the reasons these scenes are necessary is because there are so many storylines being established that it is important to keep on top of them all. Shakespeare, in a lot of his plays, doesn't have so many short scenes in quick succession. However, this play is a comedy, and an essential part of the comedy genre is a complex set of storylines and a general sense of confusion. So these scenes are there to get us on top of the action.

Act 2, Scene 3

Here we have the conversation between Jessica and Launcelot. Jessica asks Launcelot to give a letter to Lorenzo, saying:

> *'Give him this letter; do it secretly'*

This is where we establish that there is another love story; Jessica and Lorenzo are in love. It's a love story to add to the list, because we saw Gratiano, in the last scene, express some interest in accompanying Bassanio and of course he and Nerissa fall in love. So, along with Bassanio and Portia's romance, there are two other romantic storylines, emerging and developing.

This scene is really important because Jessica criticises her father. She talks about how she is:

> *'Asham'd to be my father's child!'*

She knows that it's wrong to say this:

> *'What heinous sin it is in me, to be asham'd to be my father's child'*

I think this is Shakespeare making it clear to the audience that he wants us to see Shylock as the villain, albeit a complex and very intelligent villain. If his own daughter is ashamed to be his daughter, we get the sense that he's a bad guy. This is a thread which develops and weaves throughout the whole play: good guy, bad guy, do we like him, don't we like him, should we like him? Shakespeare is expertly playing with the audiences' emotions with regards to whether we should like Shylock or not. We inevitably lean toward the negative side when his own daughter admits that she hates him.

Act 2, Scene 4

In this scene there is talk of a masked ball. Lorenzo says:

> *'Neigh, we will slink away in supper-time, disguise us at my lodging and return all in an hour'*

To which Gratiano responds:

> *'We have not spoke us of yet of torch-bearers'*

Gratiano means that they haven't planned and prepared for the party.

Two key things emerge from the conversation about this party -

1. It never takes place. That's an important point and I'll go into detail further on.

2. It tells us something about Bassanio.

One of the generic conventions of comedy is disguise. The idea behind a masked ball is that you go to a party, disguised with a mask and because you are wearing a mask, you can be quite open about flirting with people.

Masked balls feature in both Romeo and Juliet and Much ado About Nothing.

This theme of deception, of disguise, of dressing up and pretending to be somebody you're not, is in some ways foreshadowing what's going to happen later with Portia. But it's also interesting to consider why this party never actually takes place. Critics are divided as to whether Shakespeare initially intended to include a masked ball in the play and then later changed his mind and trimmed out those scenes or, alternatively, that he always intended to merely talk about a masked ball. It seems strange that there is this conversation about planning for a party that never actually takes place.

In the same scene Lorenzo says:

> *'I must need to tell thee all, she hath directed how I should take her from her father's house, what gold and jewels she's furnished with, what page's suit she hath in readiness'.*

Lorenzo is going to go and fetch Jessica, and she's going to dress up as a man. This foreshadows what's going to happen later, because we know that this idea of a woman dressing up as a man is an essential part of the storyline. We learn here that Lorenzo is going to run away with Shylock's daughter and his money. From what we already know about Shylock, we can tell, as an audience, that this will cause a lot of conflict. We might even start to put the pieces together and anticipate his outrage and subsequent lack of mercy for Antonio.

Act 2 Scene 5

Shylock is talking to his daughter, Jessica. He's about to leave the house, but he says:

> *'There is some ill a-brewing towards my rest, for I did dream of money bags tonight'*

He's essentially predicting the future, which is something he has already done at the opening of the play. He's predicting that something's going to go wrong.

This then is an upward turn for the character of Shylock. We start to think that although he may be disliked by everybody he is clearly a clever man.

He is, of course, correct. Jessica is keen to get him out of the house because she wants to escape. . But then Launcelot comes in and nearly gives the whole plot away. Launcelot says:

> *'They have conspired together'.*

This causes the audience to panic that Launcelot is about to betray Jessica and Lorenzo's plans to run away together. Launcelot, however, changes tack and moves off the topic, going on to talk about a masked ball. That really frustrates Shylock.

Shylock says:

> *'What, are these masques? Hear you me, Jessica; Lock up my doors...Clamber not you up the casement then, Nor thrust your head into the public street. '(The casement is the window.)*

Shylock is saying that if there is to be a masked ball it will inevitably be licentious and disgusting. He therefore wants Jessica to lock the doors tight and not to look out of the windows.

This is interesting because it not only establishes the controlling nature of Shylock over his daughter, but also his sense of morals and standards about which he is very passionate. He is a controlling father, and he is strong in his opinions regarding right and wrong.

This, of course, is all dramatic irony. Dramatic irony is when something takes place on the stage, about which the audience knows more than the characters themselves do. We, as an audience, know that actually Jessica is going to be leaving. Shylock is keen to tell her to stay indoors to protect herself, but we the audience know that she has already planned in to run away.

This scene is all about developing the character of Shylock. It reveals him as a controlling father, although very intelligent. The dichotomy between whether we like him or not is always present. One of the key things about drama is the effect on the audience. Shakespeare is a master at creating tension and we have this line quite near the end of the scene:

> *'Perhaps I will return immediately'*

Shylock is going out, and whilst he's gone Jessica is going to escape to run away with Lorenzo. Then Shylock says that he'll be coming straight back! You can imagine the audience taking a sharp intake of breath and panicking that he's going to come back and thwart Jessica and Lorenzo's plans.

Act 2 Scene 6

This scene is about Gratiano, Salarino, Lorenzo and eventually Jessica.

Jessica, when she enters, is wearing boy's clothes. She is above, on a balcony. This is similar to the *Romeo and Juliet* balcony scene. Shakespeare seems to favour these scenes where the woman is above the man. This is symbolic use of staging to suggest the superiority of women. When somebody is situated above somebody else, they have to look up to them which is a sign of respect, as in the expression 'to look up to someone'. That is something which we develop as children, because when we are children we literally look up to adults, physically, because they are taller than us. This is how it has become established as a sign of respect. Similarly, the opposite term is 'looking down on someone'.

So Jessica comes in above, very much like Juliet in the balcony scene in *Romeo and Juliet;* this is to establish the idea of female superiority. She is wearing boy's clothes, which develops this ongoing theme of disguise. This of course points to what Portia will eventually do. The scene takes place at night, and Jessica says:

> *'I am glad 'tis night, you do not look on me.'*

Jessica is saying that she is glad it's night-time as she doesn't want Lorenzo to see her dressed up as a boy, as she is embarrassed.

The night-time balcony scene in Romeo and Juliet was a similar scenario. Juliet, unaware that Romeo was listening to her as she talked to herself about how much she loved him, expressed her gratitude that it was night-time because the darkness hid her shame and blushes.

Shakespeare was quite keen on setting love and romance scenes at night-time. You can think for yourself about the symbolic meaning of that, but often moments of love are set at night.

Lorenzo, still thinking of the party, says:

> *'Descend, for you must be my torchbearer'*

The idea is that they can go to the party with Jessica dressed as a man, carrying the torch, so that she will be inconspicuous. But this is a party which never happens. The reason it never happens is fleetingly mentioned by Antonio who says:

> *'No masks tonight, the wind has come about'*

Antonio is saying that the party is cancelled because the wind is up.

This is interesting because it reveals something about the character of Bassanio who, as I've mentioned before, is already established as a bit of a wasteful character. We see that after all of his plans for the party, he has cancelled it. This would have been an expensive bit of planning, but he let's go of the expensive party plans so easily. This reveals the character of Bassanio to be wasteful. It's interesting that Antonio, who is footing the bill for the party, is the person who tells us that it is cancelled. You could also say that the weather ('the wind has come about') is significant, because it's hinting that a storm is on the way.

Of course there was no wind machine in Elizabethan England, which is why the character of Antonio has to tell the audience that it is windy.

Act 2, Scene 7

We see Morocco come to choose one of the caskets. The prince of Morocco had earlier been talking to Portia and it was made clear that Portia didn't want Morocco for a husband. There was a racist comment made about him, but also it was made clear that Portia wanted Bassanio. At this point the audience is emotionally invested. The Elizabethan audience at the time would have looked at this black character and been certain that they didn't want him to win Portia's hand.

Then Portia says:

> *'The one of them contains my picture, Prince; if you choose that, then I am yours withal'*

Portia is telling Morocco that if he picks the casket which contains her picture, then she is his.

Shakespeare is writing this line for the audience's benefit. Morocco and Portia know the story, but Shakespeare is always aware of his audience, and he knows that there are people in the crowd of varying levels of intelligence and concentration spans who may be watching and wondering what's happening here. These lines are for the audience's benefit as Portia is making what's going on perfectly clear.

Shakespeare then uses structure for effect. The speech that Morocco gives is one of the longest we've seen in the play so far. The audience is waiting for the moment where Morocco chooses the casket. Deep down, with this being a comedy and the expectation of a happy ending, we know he isn't going to be successful. However, Shakespeare heightens the tension and gives Morocco this incredibly long speech, which is simply there to create suspense. We can imagine Morocco moving backwards and forwards on the stage, giving this huge speech, even including a pause for dramatic effect and the audience just desperate for him to get on with it.

This is one of the ways that Shakespeare uses structure. When you're analysing structure you shouldn't just write about the structure of the play as a whole and how scenes occur next to each other - the juxtaposition of tense scenes and comic scenes to build suspense and the use of lots of very short scenes for effect. You should also analyse the structure within a scene, such as this overly long speech of Morocco's. The text is about 50 lines long. This structure builds tension and anticipation in the audience.

There is also mention here of gold. Gold is mentioned frequently throughout the play, not just in the Portia storyline but also in the obsession with wealth we see in Shylock. There is a message that wealth is not important, and we see of course that Morocco is looking at the golden casket. He opens the golden casket and discovers that it's the wrong one. He says:

> *'They have in England a coin that bears the figure of an angel stamped in gold, but here an angel in a golden bed lies all within. Deliver me the key, I choose and thrive as I may'.*

He chooses gold because he is thinking of coins and monetary value. There is a recurring theme of material wealth, and characters who are obsessed with it. However, the message is clear; material wealth is of no value. This is demonstrated when Morocco chooses a casket based on the notion of wealth and it isn't the right one.

This view of material wealth having no value is opposed to Shylock's view that money is everything. In the two different storylines, the Portia storyline seems to be establishing the idea that financial wealth isn't important. That is opposed to the Shylock storyline, where money is all he seems to care about. Even in the next scene where he loses both his daughter and his money he seems to be far more distressed about the loss of his money than the loss of his daughter!

That is quite a clear moral and message in the play, but the challenge is Bassanio. We are still unclear as to the reason why Bassanio wants to marry Portia. Is it love or is it just for her money? Why does he feel he has to dress up and pretend that he's somebody he isn't? It's almost as if he's trying to dupe Portia into the marriage, which will ultimately make him very rich. It's an interesting dilemma that we have in the play.

Morocco chooses incorrectly. He chooses a 'carry of death'.

There is a skull in his casket and he leaves. Then we have this shocking line at the end:

> *'Let all of his complexion choose me so'*

Portia is saying that she hopes that any suitor who is black chooses incorrectly.

This is another example of the overt racism that was prevalent at the time. It's an easy way to gain marks if you write about how the different contexts to the play lead to different perceptions. In Shakespeare's time they wouldn't have blinked an eye at casual racism, but today we find it uncomfortable. The patriarchal, male dominated, women-as-possessions society was very much the accepted way in Elizabethan England, but today we find it difficult to comprehend.

To achieve those high grades, you need to talk about alternative interpretations; this could mean this, but it could also mean that. One way to achieve that is to write about how two different audiences would respond to this play. The beauty of Shakespeare is that he was writing five-hundred years ago and things were so different then. Therefore, if you can write about the way we would react now compared to how we would have reacted then, you're giving appropriate alternative interpretation and context.

Act 2 Scene 8

Salarino and Solanio enter. Just as they did in scene one, they take the role of a chorus. A chorus comes onto the stage to tell the audience what has happened off-stage. We see a chorus in *Romeo and Juliet* and many other plays. They are there to ensure that the audience is keeping up with the storyline. The chorus tells you things that have happened, which is useful because it means that not everything has to actually take place on stage. You really don't need to see everything take place. The chorus says:

> *'The villain Jew with outcries rais'd the Duke, who went with him to search Bassanio's ship'*

So we're told that when Shylock discovered that his daughter and his money were gone, he was so outraged that he went to the law officials and searched the ship belonging to Bassanio, to try to find his daughter and his money. That doesn't happen on stage, it happens offstage. It's the same in Act 1, Scene 1 where Salarino and Solanio say:

> *'Your mind is tossing on the ocean,*
>
> *There, where your argosies with portly sail,*
>
> *Like signors and rich burghers on the flood—*
>
> *Do overpeer the petty traffickers'*

The chorus were used in Act 1, Scene 1 to establish that Antonio had ships at sea which contained all of his money and all of his assets. They are used again in this scene to let the audience know what's been happening. This is another structural device. This play has several storylines and a lot happening and so Shakespeare, at regular intervals, clarifies the progress of the story to us by using the chorus to update us. It is quite a confusing play, with so many storylines and people in love, that we need a bit of assistance.

We then have this well-known line where Solanio is telling us what Shylock was saying:

> *'My daughter! O my ducats! O my daughter!'*

What can we infer from this? He is equally upset at losing his money as he is his daughter! Both of the losses outrage him. By putting the two together in a sentence, it almost suggests that they are of the same value to him. Just like his money, his daughter is a possession to him. He owns her just as he owns his money.

It's interesting because Bassanio is also obsessed with money. His first impression of Portia was that she was:

> *'a lady richly left'*

Bassanio notes, first and foremost, that Portia is a rich woman, and here, Shylock too is focused on money. So although Shylock is seen as the villain and Bassanio the hero, the two of them share an unhealthy obsession with money.

We hear that Shylock said:

> *'Fled with a Christian! O my Christian ducats! Justice! The law! My ducats and my daughter! A sealed bag, two sealed bags of double ducats stolen from me by my daughter! And jewels! Two stones! Two rich and precious stones!'*

Shylock is clearly focused, to the point of obsession, on the financial element of what has gone missing. This reveals a materialistic attitude, but we lack a neat answer or conclusion because we know that Bassanio is just the same.

Then tension builds as Shylock says:

> *'Let good Antonio look he keep his day, or he shall pay for this'*

It now becomes clear that Shylock is the villain and, fuelled by his religious hatred, ('Fled with a Christian! My Christian ducats'), he hopes to exact revenge on a Christian. Shakespeare's use of the religious element makes this a bigger issue. It's not just a personal grudge between two people, it now comes across as religious hatred which would have outraged the Elizabethan audience.

Act 2 Scene 9

This scene takes us back to Portia. The alternating structure raises the tension as we have two different storylines taking place and we just want to get back to the other one to see what is going to happen.
Portia is visited by the prince of Arragon . Shakespeare is using world-play here. The name Arragon is very similar to the word arrogant. Names are often important in Shakespeare's works, although not every name has a symbolic or hidden meaning. Arragon says:

> *'Fortune now to my heart's hope, gold, silver, and base-lead. Who chooses me must give and hazard all he hath. You shall look fairer ere I give or hazard. What says the golden chest? Ha-let me see. Who chooses me shall gain what many men desire.'*

There is a sense that he isn't really interested in Portia herself. He appears to be more interested in the challenge and in winning. Then he shows himself to be the very epitome of arrogance when he says:

> *'Because I will not jump with common spirits and rank me with the barbarous multitudes'*

Revealing himself to be proud, he is saying that because most people like gold, he won't choose it, because he is not like most people.

He does come across as arrogant, just as his name suggests. He goes on to choose the silver casket, and Portia then delivers an important line, as an aside. (An aside is a line which is delivered to the audience but is not heard by the characters on stage).

Portia's aside is:

> *'Too long a pause for that which you find there'*

I believe that in the last few scenes the character of Portia has been undermined. We might have forgotten the fact that she's really intelligent and headstrong and a great woman. All we've seen is the men who want her and over whom she exerts no power. If she is established as being powerless, then we need a reminder that she is bright and intuitive. This line serves as a reminder of Portia's intelligence. She's observing that, having opened the casket, Arragon has gone quiet for a couple of seconds. She immediately realises that he isn't seeing what he wants to see. It's Shakespeare's way of reminding us that although she is at the whim of these men, she is still very intelligent. She may be subject to these men, but she doesn't deserve to be.

In Portia's final line of the scene she says:

> *'Thus hath the candle sing'd the moth. O, these deliberate fools! When they do choose they have the wisdom by their wit to lose'*

Portia is criticising these men, saying that the over intellectualising, in which they engage whilst trying to decide, actually leads them to choose the wrong caskets.

Analysis of Act 3

Act Three, Scenes One and Two

Salarino and Solanio are back. They are here to, once again, function as nothing more than a glorified chorus.

They are talking about the Rialto. The Rialto is a real bridge in Venice and it is the centre of business. Solanio says:

'What news on the Rialto?'

He's essentially asking what's going on in the world of business.

As they are the chorus, they are here to tell us what we haven't seen on stage. We're told about Antonio:

'He hath lost a ship'

It's interesting that a playwright of Shakespeare's calibre chose not to have the shipwreck scene take place on stage. This would have been a great moment of drama. Instead the chorus tell us the news.

It seems that Salarino and Solanio often, when they take on the role of chorus, tell us of big events and moments of great action which we might be disappointed we don't get to see. This is because Shakespeare wants us to focus on the main themes of justice, the way we treat people, attitudes to women, and love. So when it comes to writing about the structure, you can write not just about what happens but also about what doesn't happen or isn't included.

Shylock then comes in and says:

'I say my daughter is my flesh and blood'

This is a link to parental control. In Elizabethan England daughters were the possession of their fathers. When they married they became the possession of their husbands. Women were just there to gratify the desires and needs of men. They couldn't vote, they couldn't work, and they had inferior educations. Attitudes to women then, were so different that Shylock is saying something which all fathers in Elizabethan England would have thought.

There is a sense of possession in:

'She is my flesh and blood'.

This is relevant because it's not:

'She's from my flesh and blood'.

He is saying that she acts as a reflection on him. We get the sense that Shylock is quite proud.

Then we move on to this significant speech which is so well known. Shylock says:

'If it will feed nothing else, it will feed my revenge'

Shylock is being honest here. He's saying that the deal he's struck with Antonio will, if nothing else, allow Shylock to have revenge.

There's no dishonesty in the character of Shylock, but we see much dishonesty in other characters. Launcelot pretends to be someone else to his father, Old Gobbo, and tells him that his son is dead. Later in the play, characters dress in disguise to deceive others. Bassanio and Antonio promise to keep their rings but proceed to give them away. So much of this play is filled with lies and deceit, and yet Shylock is honest. He's one of those people who we wish wasn't quite so shockingly honest.

Shylock is being honest when he announces that he's going to get his revenge and that's that.

Then follows Shylock's well- known speech:

> *'I am a Jew. Hath not a Jew eyes? Hath not a Jew hands? Organs? Dimensions? Senses? Affections? Passions? Fed with the same food? Hurt with the same weapons? Subject to the same diseases? Healed by the same means? Warmed and cooled by the same winter and summer as a Christian is? If you prick us, do we not bleed? If you tickle us, do we not laugh?'*

This is a plea for human tolerance. There is no response to Shylock's questions. His listeners are silenced. They cannot argue back. Shakespeare has, here, given the character of Shylock such a powerful, emotive speech and even though he is a villain, it evokes sympathy in the audience. It causes us to wonder whether we are supposed to like Shylock or not. The truth is that it hangs in the balance whether we like Shylock or not. At this moment we can't help but feel sorry for him and perhaps it causes us to consider how easily we are drawn towards disliking Shylock and then questioning our attitude.

This speech represents a turning point for the character of Shylock mid-way through the play. However, look at the structural significance of the very next thing he says:

> *'A diamond gone, cost me two thousand ducats in Frankfort!'*

Just as we start to have feelings of sympathy for the character of Shylock, they disappear again because he's ranting about his loss of money. We know that he's lost his daughter as well as some money, but he seems to be more preoccupied with his financial loss. He appears to be materialistic. His callous materialism extinguishes the sympathy that has just been re-ignited in our hearts by Shakespeare. If we were to draw a graph of the emotions we feel towards Shylock, it would be constantly peaking and troughing. We're unsure how we should feel about him. It's clear from the way Shakespeare ends his play that Shylock is treated as a villain, and he loses everything, his money, his family, his religion, in a shocking turn of events.

Shylock says a disturbing thing in the speech:

> *'I would my daughter were dead at my foot'*

He's wishing his daughter dead because she ran away with some of his money and a Christian man! This reveals him to be a thoroughly unlikeable character.

Act 3 Scene 2

Portia delivers a long speech to Bassanio. We see long speeches in other parts of the play, but this one is noteable because it is nonsensical:

> *'I pray you, tarry. Pause a day or two*
> *Before you hazard, for in choosing wrong*
> *I lose your company. Therefore forbear awhile*

There's something tells me – But it's not love -
I would not lose you, and you know yourself
Hate counsels not in such a quality.
But lest you should not understand me well-
And yet a maiden hath no tongue but thought-
I would detain you here some month or two
Before you venture for me. I could teach you
How to choose right, but I am then forsworn.
So I will never be. So may you miss me.
But if you do, you'll make me wish a sin,
That I had been forsworn. Beshrew your eyes,
They have o'erlooked me and divided me.
One half of me is yours, the other half yours-
Mine own, I would say. But if mine, then yours,
and so all yours. Oh, these naughty times
Put bars between the owners and their rights!
And so, though yours, not yours. Prove it so.
Let fortune go to hell for, not I.
I speak too long, but 'tis to Prize the time,
To eke it and to draw it out in length
To stay you from election.'

This speech is full of random interjected thoughts. It is chaotic. The Portia we see at this moment is in contrast to the Portia we see in the rest of the play. In Acts 1 and 2 Portia is presented as a witty wordsmith who is able to deliver brilliant lines of argument and double-meanings. Yet here we are presented with a Portia who is unable to even string her ideas together. This is a nonsensical speech.

The ridiculousness of Portia's speech is heightened by the fact that it comes just after Shylock's brilliant, eloquent speech. That's another structural device: the juxtaposition of two long speeches which reveal a lot about the characters. In this example Portia comes out lacking.

We need to ask ourselves why Portia's speech is so atypical and erratic. One explanation is that love has changed her. She has fallen in love with Bassanio and her emotions are out of control.

I recently read the autobiography of the comedian Dom Jolly, who recounted that he occasionally bumps into musicians from his favourite rock groups, who were his childhood heroes. He explained that, during these encounters, he becomes so overawed that he can't speak coherently. He says that he talks utter rubbish, and that is exactly what we're witnessing here with Portia. Shakespeare uses language, in the deliberate confusion and nonsensical nature of Portia's speech, to establish that something has changed. The thing that has changed is that Portia has fallen in love with Bassanio. What does it say about love though? It seems to suggest that love makes you lose your intelligence. It's also interesting to note that in this speech Portia says:

'One half of me is yours, the other half yours – Mine own I would say, then yours, and so all yours.'

There's a suggestion here about the role of women, being at the mercy of men and dependant on them making right choices.

Once again we come back to the fact that although Portia is witty and intelligent and rich, she is ultimately still subject to the men around her and the choices they make.

We have this prolonged, chaotic, elaborate and nonsensical speech in which Portia openly admits that she loves Bassanio and strongly desires him to choose the right casket and to stay there for months. She ultimately opens her heart to Bassanio and he responds:

> *'Let me choose for as I am, I live upon the rack.'*

This is a short, blunt denial. Bassanio is saying that he isn't going to stay a couple of months before he chooses, that it is really hard for him and he just wants to get on with it.

He doesn't reciprocate with a long, extravagant speech, or make himself vulnerable and open up his heart to Portia, or justify what he says. Instead he is blunt and to the point. This demonstrates the inequality and differing expectations of behaviour and attitude that existed between men and women in Elizabethan England. He is not even particularly polite despite the fact that Portia is of far higher status than he.

Whilst Bassanio is looking at the caskets, pondering them and deciding which to choose, a song is sung. The stage directions say:

> *'A song, that whilst Bassanio comments on the caskets to himself'.*

This is the first time in the play that a song has been sung whilst a suitor is choosing his casket. Arragon, the previous suitor, was given a long speech and this served to heighten tension in the audience as they waited for him to make his choice. Now we have a song, a deliberate structural choice by Shakespeare because he wants to prolong this moment and further ratchet up the tension. The audience is desperate for Bassanio to choose quickly as we have been anticipating this moment since the beginning of the play.

Later there is an inter-textual reference to Midas. Midas was the mythical king who was granted his wish that everything he touched would turn to gold. Ultimately he starved to death because whenever he touched food, it turned to gold and he couldn't eat it. The granting of his wish led to his ultimate demise. In this play, Shylock is the metaphorical Midas because, like Midas, he believes that gold and wealth is to be valued above all else. The message of the play is that wealth is only useful for helping in the pursuit of love, and the reality is that Shylock doesn't understand that.

The inter-textual references in the play are cleverly thought through by Shakespeare.

When eventually Bassanio makes the right choice, Portia says:

> *'Myself and what is mine to you and yours*
> *Is now converted. But now I was the lord*
> *of this fair mansion...*
> *This house, these servants, and this same myself,*
> *Are yours – my lord's. I give them with this ring,'*

The ring will, of course, be important later. However, here the contextual role of women is laid bare. Everything Portia has is now Bassanio's, including herself. When a woman married, she and everything she owned, became the actual physical property of her husband. At this point we are only in Act 3, Scene 2 and everything seems to be coming together nicely.

It is important now, structurally, that Shakespeare causes something to happen that will further the plot. This requirement is fulfilled when a letter from Antonio is brought to Bassanio. The letter informs us that Antonio has lost everything. His whole fleet of ships has been shipwrecked and therefore all of his wealth has been lost. Antonio tells Bassanio that he knows Shylock will take his 'pound of flesh' and that as a result of this Antonio will die. Antonio expresses that his dearest wish is that he sees his good friend Bassanio again before he dies.

Shakespeare's plot device ensures that the drama continues and deepens.

Act Three, Scenes Three and Four

Scene 3 takes place in a street in Venice. Shylock, Salarino, and Antonio enter. Shylock says that he wants to exact his revenge and take his bond from Antonio:

> *'I'll have my bond; speak not against my bond. I have sworn an oath that I will have my bond.'*

Here Shakespeare is using a language technique. He is using the rule of three and also the repetition of the word 'bond' and the phrase 'my bond'. Repetition is one of the language devices often employed by Shakespeare to show obsession. Shylock is obsessed now with taking his revenge on Antonio and claiming his 'pound of flesh' by lawfully exacting his bond. Antonio resigns himself to the, seemingly, inevitable outcome.

Shylock says:

> *'Since I am a dog, beware my fangs'*

This is another use of clever word-play from Shakespeare. It is often the minority characters and the weaker characters who are empowered by Shakespeare with intelligent and clever use of language. The minorities in this play are Jews and women - Shylock and Portia. Shakespeare appears to be endorsing an early form of feminism in his treatment of the character Portia. He wants women to be treated with more respect and so he often empowers his female characters. However, we are unsure of Shakespeare's attitude towards Shylock and whether he wants, on occasion, to empower him too. There are times when Shylock is built up to be some sort of hero, before being brought right back down to earth and shown to be a villain. There is a dilemma in our perception of Shylock at times – victim/victor/villain? We wonder what Shakespeare is trying to say about Jews. Is he advocating that we should be more respectful to Jews, in a time where there was no respect for Jews? Shylock is clearly intent on retaliating for the ill-treatment he's received as a result of being Jewish:

> *'Since I am a dog, beware my fangs'*

Shylock is saying that the way he has been ill-treated will have repercussions because he is going to react appropriately.

The clever word-play hints at the fact the Shakespeare has a lot of respect for both Portia and Shylock.

This short scene ends with Antonio making it very clear that he realises and accepts the inevitability of his plight:

> *'The duke cannot deny the course of law for the commodity that strangers have with us in Venice, if it be denied will much impeach the justice of the state'*

Antonio is saying that he realises that because he lives in Venice, the centre for commercial business, the law must be seen to be upheld, otherwise it would be detrimental to Venice's reputation as a trading centre.

The Venetian setting is significant because Venice is a place where the letter of the law has to be adhered to. The whole city strictly adheres to the letter of the law, because there is so much international business which takes place there.

If Shakespeare had set this play in a different city and Shylock was resolute about enforcing the letter of the law on Antonio, it would have no far reaching repercussions if the duke pardoned him. However, because the setting is Venice, an Elizabethan audience would understand that it is the international commercial hub of the country and absolute compliance with the law would be expected. Faith in a just legal system of integrity would otherwise be undermined and businesses would hesitate to carry out commercial transactions in such a corrupt city.

The Elizabethan audience held Venice in a different level of respect to contemporary audiences. Today we might just think of Venice as a holiday destination. So Shakespeare's use of setting here is very important. Many of Shakespeare's plays are set in locations where the story originated from. For example *Romeo and Juliet* is set in Verona because the original story on which Shakespeare based the play [supposedly a true story] is a story from Verona. In many cases Shakespeare had no choice of the setting because the locations were decided in the original stories. That's not to say that Shakespeare didn't write the plays but rather that some of his plays had a literary influence from beforehand.

There are a couple of important things to note about *The Merchant of Venice;* the play has Jewish characters in it and therefore it couldn't be set in the UK because there were no Jews in England at that time. The setting of Venice works very well because it is the location for the hub of business, which is so important in this play. It's also significant in helping us understand just why it is that Shylock is so angry and adamant that Antonio abides by the Venetian laws. Shylock is angry with Antonio because Antonio is ruining his business by lending money without charging interest. This is detrimental to Shylock because he is a money lender. Shylock can't make a profit lending money if there is a Christian whose beliefs lead him to lend money without charging interest.

There are several texts which may have influenced *The Merchant of Venice*. There is an Italian tale called *Il Pecorone* or *The simpleton* which was written in 1378 and it is thought that it was an influence on this play. In that story, a wealthy woman at Belmont marries an upstanding young gentleman. Her husband needs money, and a friend desperate to help goes to a money lender. The money lender, a Jew, demands a pound of flesh as payment. So we can see that this story was Italian in origin.

This isn't to say that Shakespeare was stealing ideas. It's not the case at all. It was well known that he didn't always come up with the original storylines; he took these ideas and turned them into plays. He also added minor characters. The reason that the settings for the stories work so well is because they are based on true stories or stories which are believed to be true.

In Act 3 scenes 3 and 4 we have a long speech by Lorenzo, Shylock is demanding his pound of flesh and Antonio is resigning himself to the inevitability of forfeiting it, in order to fulfil the requirements of the law.

This is a huge, climactic moment and here, Shakespeare chooses to change the structure of the play and introduce another pacing scene. We have this moment of great tension is scene 3, and here in scene 4 we change to a different storyline; Lorenzo and Portia are having a conversation, along with Jessica and Balthazar. Once more Shakespeare's brilliant use of structure leaves us hungry for more and desperate to find out Antonio's plight.

There are one or two things of interest in this scene. One of them is this speech from Lorenzo:

'Madam, although I speak it in your presence,

You have a noble and true conceit

Of godlike amity, which appears most strongly

In bearing thus the absence of your lord.

But if you knew to whom you show this honor,

How true a gentleman you send relief,

How dear a lover of my lord your husband,

I know you would be prouder of the work

Than customary bounty can enforce you.'

Here we find Lorenzo linking Portia to Antonio because the two of them have no connection at this point in the play. Lorenzo is commending Antonio to Portia. Portia wants to free Antonio, her husband's friend. Friendship was often a theme in Elizabethan plays. In fact, it's argued that friendship was as important in Elizabethan England as romance and love. It's clear, then, that Portia is motivated to help out. We finish with Portia saying to Nerissa:

'When we are both accoutred like young men'

Portia has a plan for the two of them to dress up as young men. This continues the themes of disguise and deception which we see throughout the play.

Act Three, Scene Five

We're now approaching the end of the play. Scene 5 is another humorous scene which is interesting because, structurally, Shakespeare has decided to put this light hearted, comical scene in, not because the previous scene was so depressing, dramatic and serious, but because the next scene in the courtroom is so serious. Throughout the play we have to remind ourselves that this is not a Shakespearian tragedy where someone is going to die at the end. It is a comedy, even though it is a rather dark comedy at times. Here Shakespeare is warming up the audience for what is about to follow in Act 4, Scene 1 which is an incredibly long, serious and focused scene.

So we have some humour throughout this scene with Jessica, Lorenzo, Launcelot, and some jokes that would have really made the audience laugh. Lorenzo says:

'I shall grow jealous of you shortly, Launcelot, if you thus get my wife into corners.'

However, he is told by Jessica:

'Nay, you need not fear us, Lorenzo. Launcelot and I are in out. He tells me flatly there's no mercy for me in heaven because I am a Jew's daughter, and he says you are no good member of the commonwealth for in converting Jews to Christians you raise the price of pork.'

This would be entertaining to the audience, because they would be aware that Jews do not eat pork, and therefore every time a Jew becomes a Christian the amount of people eating pork will increase. The greater demand for pork would therefore drive up the price. It's very much a joke, but it's interesting to note that the joke is couched in the terms of business transactions and industry which is a crucial element of the play.

This scene takes place in Belmont, where Jessica is now living. Belmont is run by women, but that's acceptable because it's situated away from the town centre. Women could run country houses which were in isolated locations. Jessica has gone from Shylock's home to Belmont which is a symbolic journey that she's undertaken and it has had a really positive effect on her. She is revealed to be very witty and intelligent in this scene which demonstrates that she's becoming like Portia. This demonstrates Shakespeare's fondness for presenting women as having great strengths when they're not under the domineering control of men.

Analysis of Act 4

Act 4, Scene 1

This is a very interesting scene because it is the tense courtroom scene, but it also culminates in the happy ending that is demanded by a romantic comedy play. We start this scene with the Duke, Antonio, Bassanio, Salarino, Gratiano and some others. The Duke is talking to Antonio, saying:

> *'I am sorry for thee; thou art come to answer*
> *A stony adversary, and inhuman wretch,*
> *Incapable of pity, void and empty*
> *From every dram of mercy.'*

It's amazing how much emotive language is used here, by Shakespeare, to paint an incredibly negative picture of Shylock: 'Stony, inhuman wretch, void, empty.' He uses an overload of negative language to make it absolutely clear that Shylock is now an out and out villain. We've been unsure throughout the play how to interpret his character, alternating between anger towards him, sympathy for him, positive perceptions of him which are consistently, quickly dispelled by negative perceptions of him. We've been angry, then sympathetic, then positive, then negative. But here the plethora of negative language used by Shakespeare is very clearly establishing that he is the villain.

Antonio says:

> *'I have heard*
> *Your Grace hath ta'en great pains to qualify his rigorous course'*

Antonio is acknowledging that, although the Duke is trying to reason with Shylock to convince him to change his heart and not to follow through with his outrageous demand for a pound of flesh, he realises that Shylock is unrelenting in his planned course of action.

This sets the scene beautifully because we know that Portia is on her way to save the day. Shakespeare is saying that it's impossible for even the wisest of men to win over Shylock. This gives us hope that maybe Portia will succeed where others have failed.

Shylock says:

> *'If you deny me, fie upon your law'*

He's supposedly motivated by a desire for justice, but we know that revenge is his true motive. Venice is the commercial centre of the country and business would be adversely affected if the law was not seen to be upheld.

There's an example of dramatic irony when Shylock says:

> *'There is no power in the tongue of man to alter me.'*

Shylock is asserting that no man can dissuade him from taking his pound of flesh from Antonio. Whilst this may be true, we know that Portia is on her way, disguised as a man, and she will thwart Shylock's evil intentions.

The tension continues to soar as Portia, disguised as a lawyer, says:

> *'You must prepare your bosom for his knife'*

You can imagine the audience panicking, wondering what on earth is going to happen next.

Then Portia very cleverly leads Shylock into a trap. She asks him questions which are designed to ultimately lead to his downfall. In the end Portia, disguised as the lawyer, frees him.

Bassanio then delivers a revelatory speech, completely unaware that his wife is actually present in the court room, disguised as a man, listening to him:

'Antonio, I am married to a wife
Which is as dear to me as life itself;
But life itself, my wife, and all the world,
Are not with me esteem'd above thy life:
I would lose all, ay, sacrifice them all
Here to this devil, to deliver you.'

Gratiano then delivers a similar speech:

'I have a wife, who, I protest, I love:
I would she were in heaven, so she could
Entreat some power to change this currish Jew.'

In these two speeches we see very clearly the Elizabethan attitude to women. The women are clearly not regarded as highly as men. Both Bassanio and Gratiano say that they would give their wives' lives if it would save Antonio!

Then Portia, using the intelligence which she has displayed throughout the play, works out how to save Antonio. She says:

'Tarry a little; there is something else.
This bond doth give thee here no jot of blood;
The words expressly are 'a pound of flesh:'
Take then thy bond, take thou thy pound of flesh;
But, in cutting it, if thou dost shed
One drop of Christian blood, thy lands and goods
Are, by the laws of Venice, confiscate
Unto the city of Venice.'

It is left to Portia to thwart Shylock's evil intention. Antonio, Bassanio and the Duke have all tried and failed to find a way to do so. Portia then arrives, saves the day and presents a very strong moral to the play regarding society's laws. Portia makes it clear that law needs to be tempered with mercy, otherwise it can lead to evil. The play reveals that law alone is not good enough. We go on to see the harsh treatment of Shylock, but it's interesting to think about the contextual information.

Shylock is told that he must become a Christian. To us today it seems a dreadful thing to force someone to abandon their religion and to adopt another one. However, the Elizabethan audience might think of this a bit differently because they would believe, as the bible says, that the only way to heaven is through Jesus. They would think that by forcing him to become a Christian, they were actually saving Shylock from going to hell.

It's an interesting scene, and we can see why it was preceded by a comic scene. So much happens in Act 4, Scene 1.

Act Four, Scene Two to End

Act 4, Scene 2

This is a humorous scene. We have Portia talking to Nerissa, saying:

'We'll outface them, and outswear them too.'

Once again we have here an example of female characters engaging in verbal battle with male characters. There is a serious point being made here by Shakespeare, because, once again, his female characters outwit the male characters. This is something we see repeatedly in the comedy of William Shakespeare. He empowers the female characters with clever jokes and intelligent lines which could lead us to interpret Shakespeare as an early feminist. This is all the more surprising considering the prevailing attitude towards women in Elizabethan England.

Analysis of Act 5

Act 5, Scene 1

This scene takes place at night in Belmont, and Lorenzo and Jessica are in the garden of Portia's house.

Lorenzo says:

'The moon shines bright.
In such a night as this.
When the sweet wind did
gently kiss the trees and
they did make no noise,
in such a night...'

In both this play and in *Romeo and Juliet*, night time is a setting for romance. Just by introducing the setting of night time, it causes the audience to anticipate a romantic scene. This is a generic convention with which Elizabethan audiences would have been familiar.

Although this is a romantic scene, that doesn't preclude it from containing a lot of humour too. There is a long conversation between Nerissa and Gratiano. Part of it contains irony when Nerissa says:

'Gave it a judge's clerk! No, God's my judge.
The clerk would never wear hair on's face that had it'

This is ironic because Nerissa knows that she is the judge's clerk and she'll never have hair on her face because she's a woman. Then, there's a funny exchange where Gratiano says:

'Now by this hand, I gave it to a youth.

A kind of boy, a little scrubbed boy

No higher than thyself, the judges clerk.

A pratting boy that begged it as a fee.'

He's being very critical of the clerk, totally unaware that Nerissa was in fact the clerk. This is followed by more dramatic irony as Portia says:

'You were to blame, I must be plain with you,
To part so slightly with your wife's first gift.
A thing stuck on with oaths upon your finger
And so riveted with faith upon your flesh.
I gave my love a ring and made him swear
Never to part with it. And here he stands'

This is another instance of dramatic irony, where we the audience know more than the characters on stage. You can imagine the male characters squirming as Portia and Nerissa enjoy themselves criticising the men for parting with their rings This use of dramatic irony causes the audience to side with Portia. It's another way for Shakespeare to empower his female characters. He wants us to laugh, alongside Portia and Nerissa, at the men. We, the audience are in on the joke and this causes us to feel empowered and united with Portia and Nerissa.

A little further on there is more humour relating to Portia and Bassanio's bed.

Portia says:

> *'Let not that doctor e'er come near my house!*
> *Since he hath got the jewel that I loved,*
> *And that which you did swear to keep for me,*
> *I will become as liberal as you.*
> *I'll not deny him anything I have,*
> *No, not my body, nor my husband's bed.'*

This is all humour and dramatic irony, as Portia is saying that the doctor of law to whom Bassanio gave the ring, can have her as well!

Of course, we know that the doctor of law is Portia in disguise! Naturally, Bassanio doesn't like hearing Portia say these seemingly outrageous things.

In the final moments of the play we encounter a slightly sinister undertone where Bassanio says:

> *'Portia, forgive me of this enforced wrong, and in the hearing of these many friends I swear to thee even by thine own fair eyes, Wherein I see myself'*

This is interesting because Bassanio is saying that when he looks into Portia's eyes he sees himself. This suggests that Portia is his possession now that they are married. Marriage has turned her into his possession. It is very much contrasted with what we read in Act 1, Scene 1 where Bassanio talks about Portia's eyes and says:

> *'Sometimes, from her eyes, I did receive fair, speechless messages'*

When he was wooing Portia, before he won her, Bassanio looked into her eyes and sensed that she was trying to communicate with him. Now that Portia belongs to him, through the act of marriage, he looks into her eyes and sees himself. This is a big shift from the positive description we saw in Act 1, Scene 1 and now has a quite negative and sinister undertone, suggesting that Portia is no longer her own person or an individual, but rather a reflection of himself.

This final scene contains a lot of comedy, partly to lighten the mood, but also to avoid being too romantic. There was a lot of romantic theatre in the Elizabethan period, and it was frowned upon as being gushy and insipid. Shakespeare wanted to make it clear that while there was romance in The Merchant of Venice, the intelligent word-play, witty banter, clever puns and jokes were the primary element of this play, along with some sinister undertones regarding attitudes to women, justice, racism and persecution.

Translation of Act 1 Scene 1

ORIGINAL TEXT	MODERN TRANSLATION
Venice. A street.	**A street in Venice.**
Enter ANTONIO, SALARINO, and SALANIO	*Enter ANTONIO, SALARINO, and SALANIO*
ANTONIO In sooth, I know not why I am so sad: It wearies me; you say it wearies you; But how I caught it, found it, or came by it, What stuff 'tis made of, whereof it is born, I am to learn; And such a want-wit sadness makes of me, That I have much ado to know myself.	**ANTONIO** Truthfully, I don't know why I am so sad. It drains me; you say it drains you; But how I came to feel like this, The cause or where it's come from, I don't know; And such a lack of insight regarding this sadness Makes me feel as if I don't understand myself.
SALARINO Your mind is tossing on the ocean; There, where your argosies with portly sail, Like signiors and rich burghers on the flood, Or, as it were, the pageants of the sea, Do overpeer the petty traffickers, That curtsy to them, do them reverence, As they fly by them with their woven wings.	**SALARINO:** Your thoughts are focused on the ocean; There where your ships, with grand sails - Like gentlemen and rich inhabitants of the ocean, Like a spectacular sea borne procession - Do look down on the little boats, Which politely and respectfully move out of the way, As they fly past, sails billowing.
SALANIO Believe me, sir, had I such venture forth, The better part of my affections would Be with my hopes abroad. I should be still Plucking the grass, to know where sits the wind, Peering in maps for ports and piers and roads; And every object that might make me fear Misfortune to my ventures, out of doubt Would make me sad.	**SOLANIO** Believe me, sir, if I had a business like yours, Most of my attention would Be focused on my ships at sea. I would be constantly Throwing grass into the air to find out in which direction the wind is blowing, Scrutinising maps for ports, piers and roads; And anything that caused me to worry About my ships' safety, would Definitely make me sad.
SALARINO My wind cooling my broth Would blow me to an ague, when I thought What harm a wind too great at sea might do. I should not see the sandy hour-glass run, But I should think of shallows and of flats, And see my wealthy Andrew dock'd in sand, Vailing her high-top lower than her ribs To kiss her burial. Should I go to church And see the holy edifice of stone, And not bethink me straight of dangerous rocks, Which touching but my gentle vessel's side, Would scatter all her spices on the stream, Enrobe the roaring waters with my silks,	**SALARINO** Blowing on my soup to cool it, Would give me a fever when I thought about The damage a storm at sea could do. I wouldn't be able to look at the sand flowing through an hour glass Without thinking of shallow waters and sand-bars, And imagine my valuable ship, Andrew, run aground, Listing severely As she's shipwrecked. If I went to church And looked at the building's stonework, I would think, straight away, of dangerous rocks, Which, if they damaged my ship's hull, Would cause the cargo of spices to be washed away, My silks would be thrown about in the stormy seas,

And, in a word, but even now worth this, And now worth nothing? Shall I have the thought To think on this, and shall I lack the thought That such a thing bechanced would make me sad?	One moment having wealth, And suddenly having nothing? If I think about this And ponder the possibility, can I deny That the possibility of such a disaster would make me sad?
But tell not me; I know, Antonio Is sad to think upon his merchandise.	But don't answer me; I know that Antonio is concerned for the safety of his cargo.
ANTONIO Believe me, no: I thank my fortune for it, My ventures are not in one bottom trusted, Nor to one place; nor is my whole estate Upon the fortune of this present year: Therefore my merchandise makes me not sad.	**ANTONIO** Believe me, no; I am very fortunate that, My business interests are not invested in just one ship, Nor in one country; nor is my entire wealth Dependent on doing well financially this year; So it's not my business which is making me sad.
SALARINO Why, then you are in love.	**SOLANIO** Well then, you must be in love.
ANTONIO Fie, fie!	**ANTONIO** Oh, for goodness sake!
SALARINO Not in love neither? Then let us say you are sad, Because you are not merry: and 'twere as easy For you to laugh and leap and say you are merry, Because you are not sad. Now, by two-headed Janus, Nature hath framed strange fellows in her time: Some that will evermore peep through their eyes And laugh like parrots at a bag-piper, And other of such vinegar aspect That they'll not show their teeth in way of smile, Though Nestor swear the jest be laughable.	**SOLANIO** You're not in love either? Well, let's just say you're sad Because you're not happy; and it's as easy For you to laugh and dance and say you're happy, Because you're not sad. Now, by two headed Janus, We are all so different: Some, whose eyes are always crinkled with laughter, And laugh at things which aren't even funny; And others, so sour faced That they never crack a smile No matter how funny the joke is.
Enter BASSANIO, LORENZO, and GRATIANO	*Enter BASSANIO, LORENZO, and GRATIANO*
SALANIO Here comes Bassanio, your most noble kinsman, Gratiano and Lorenzo. Fare ye well: We leave you now with better company.	**SOLANIO** Here comes Bassanio, your most admirable relative, Gratiano and Lorenzo. Good bye; We will leave you with good company.
SALARINO I would have stay'd till I had made you merry, If worthier friends had not prevented me.	**SALARINO** I would have stayed until I had cheered you up, If closer friends hadn't turned up.
ANTONIO Your worth is very dear in my regard. I take it, your own business calls on you And you embrace the occasion to depart.	**ANTONIO** I really value your friendship. I assume that you have to attend to your own business, And you're taking the opportunity to leave.
SALARINO Good morrow, my good lords.	**SALARINO** Good day, gentlemen.

BASSANIO Good signiors both, when shall we laugh? say, when? You grow exceeding strange: must it be so?	**BASSANIO** Good sirs, when shall we get together for a good laugh? You say when. We haven't met up for ages; we mustn't leave it so long, must we?
SALARINO We'll make our leisures to attend on yours. *Exeunt Salarino and Salanio*	**SALARINO** We'll fit in with your availability. *Exeunt Salarino and Salanio*
LORENZO My Lord Bassanio, since you have found Antonio, We two will leave you: but at dinner-time, I pray you, have in mind where we must meet.	**LORENZO** My Lord Bassanio, since you have Antonio's company, We two will leave you; but at dinnertime, Please don't forget where we're meeting up.
BASSANIO I will not fail you.	**BASSANIO** I won't let you down.
GRATIANO You look not well, Signior Antonio; You have too much respect upon the world: They lose it that do buy it with much care: Believe me, you are marvellously changed.	**GRATIANO** You don't look happy, Mr Antonio; You're thinking about worldly things too much; If you value worldly things too highly, you lose them. I can see that you're really not yourself.
ANTONIO I hold the world but as the world, Gratiano; A stage where every man must play a part, And mine a sad one.	**ANTONIO** To me the world is just the world, Gratiano – A stage where every man has a part to play, And my part is a sad one.
GRATIANO Let me play the fool: With mirth and laughter let old wrinkles come, And let my liver rather heat with wine Than my heart cool with mortifying groans. Why should a man, whose blood is warm within, Sit like his grandsire cut in alabaster? Sleep when he wakes and creep into the jaundice By being peevish? I tell thee what, Antonio-- I love thee, and it is my love that speaks-- There are a sort of men whose visages Do cream and mantle like a standing pond, And do a wilful stillness entertain, With purpose to be dress'd in an opinion Of wisdom, gravity, profound conceit, As who should say 'I am Sir Oracle, And when I ope my lips let no dog bark!' O my Antonio, I do know of these That therefore only are reputed wise For saying nothing; when, I am very sure, If they should speak, would almost damn those ears, Which, hearing them, would call their brothers fools.	**GRATIANO** Then I'll play the part of a fool. With merriment and fun get laughter lines; And choose to cheer myself up with wine Rather than to deny myself and be miserable. Why should a hot blooded male Act like his cold, pale grandfather, The walking dead and gradually become cynical, Through being discontented? I'm saying this Antonio – Because I love you and I'm speaking out of love for you - There are some men whose faces Appear, on the surface, like a stagnant pond, They choose to keep a straight face, In order to give the appearance Of wisdom, seriousness, and great self importance; As if to say ' I am the fount of all knowledge And when I speak not even a dog should bark'. Oh my Antonio, I know that sort That are only thought to be wise Because they say nothing; when I am convinced, That if they spoke, would shock the ears Of their listeners, who would realise that they are fools.

I'll tell thee more of this another time: But fish not, with this melancholy bait, For this fool gudgeon, this opinion. Come, good Lorenzo. Fare ye well awhile: I'll end my exhortation after dinner.	I'll talk about this with you some other time. But don't go around with this appearance of sadness And get this reputation. Come on, dear Lorenzo. Bye for now;
LORENZO Well, we will leave you then till dinner-time: I must be one of these same dumb wise men, For Gratiano never lets me speak.	**LORENZO** I'll finish my inspiring speech after dinner. I must be one of those dumb, founts of all knowledge, Because Gratiano never lets me get a word in edgeways.
GRATIANO Well, keep me company but two years moe, Thou shalt not know the sound of thine own tongue.	**GRATIANO** Well, stick with me for another couple of years, And you'll forget the sound of your own voice.
ANTONIO Farewell: I'll grow a talker for this gear.	**ANTONIO** Goodbye; This has motivated me to become talkative.
GRATIANO Thanks, i' faith, for silence is only commendable In a neat's tongue dried and a maid not vendible.	**GRATIANO** Thanks, I hope so, because silence is only appreciated From dried Ox tongue and old maids.
Exeunt GRATIANO and LORENZO	*Exeunt GRATIANO and LORENZO*
ANTONIO Is that any thing now?	**ANTONIO** Is he right?
BASSANIO Gratiano speaks an infinite deal of nothing, more than any man in all Venice. His reasons are as two grains of wheat hid in two bushels of chaff: you shall seek all day ere you find them, and when you have them, they are not worth the search.	**BASSANIO** Gratiano speaks a load of nonsense, More than anyone in the whole of Venice. Trying to understand him is like looking for a needle in a haystack: you look all day until you find it and when you do, you realise that it wasn't worth the effort.
ANTONIO Well, tell me now what lady is the same To whom you swore a secret pilgrimage, That you to-day promised to tell me of?	**ANTONIO** Well, who is this lady Whom you're determined to make a secret journey to visit, That you promised to tell me about today?
BASSANIO 'Tis not unknown to you, Antonio, How much I have disabled mine estate, By something showing a more swelling port Than my faint means would grant continuance: Nor do I now make moan to be abridged From such a noble rate; but my chief care Is to come fairly off from the great debts Wherein my time something too prodigal Hath left me gaged. To you, Antonio, I owe the most, in money and in love, And from your love I have a warranty	**BASSANIO** You know, Antonio, How much I have mismanaged my finances By owing more interest Than I can manage to keep paying; I'm not giving you a sob story to get out of This interest rate; but my main concern Is to get out of the debt Which my extravagant living, Has led to, leaving me trapped. To you Antonio, I owe the most, in money and in love; And because of your love I have assurance

To unburden all my plots and purposes How to get clear of all the debts I owe.	That I can confide in you all my plans On how to get out of debt.
ANTONIO I pray you, good Bassanio, let me know it; And if it stand, as you yourself still do, Within the eye of honour, be assured, My purse, my person, my extremest means, Lie all unlock'd to your occasions.	**ANTONIO** Please, dear Bassanio, tell me about it; And if it appears to me, as you do, To have integrity, then rest assured That my money, myself and all that I have,Are at your disposal.
BASSANIO In my school-days, when I had lost one shaft, I shot his fellow of the self-same flight The self-same way with more advised watch, To find the other forth, and by adventuring both I oft found both: I urge this childhood proof, Because what follows is pure innocence. I owe you much, and, like a wilful youth, That which I owe is lost; but if you please To shoot another arrow that self way Which you did shoot the first, I do not doubt, As I will watch the aim, or to find both Or bring your latter hazard back again And thankfully rest debtor for the first.	**BASSANIO** When I was a school boy, when I lost an arrow, I would shoot another similar arrow In the same direction, but I'd watch more carefully, Where it landed; and by shooting both of them I often found both of the arrows. I'm giving you this example from my childhood, Because what I'm about to tell you, was not done deliberately. I owe you a lot; and like a strong willed child, I lost the money I owe you; but if you're willing To shoot another arrow the same way You shot the first one, I will definitely, As I will be more careful with this investment, I will pay back your second loan And will, with great gratitude, pay off the first loan.
ANTONIO You know me well, and herein spend but time To wind about my love with circumstance; And out of doubt you do me now more wrong In making question of my uttermost Than if you had made waste of all I have: Then do but say to me what I should do That in your knowledge may by me be done, And I am prest unto it: therefore, speak.	**ANTONIO** You know me well, and you're wasting your time Thinking that your circumstances could possibly change my love for you; And by doubting that, you let me down more By being unsure of my uttermost commitment to you Than if you had bankrupted me. So just tell me what you want me to do What you think I can do to help you, And I am ready to help; so just tell me.
BASSANIO In Belmont is a lady richly left; And she is fair, and, fairer than that word, Of wondrous virtues: sometimes from her eyes I did receive fair speechless messages: Her name is Portia, nothing undervalued To Cato's daughter, Brutus' Portia: Nor is the wide world ignorant of her worth, For the four winds blow in from every coast Renowned suitors, and her sunny locks Hang on her temples like a golden fleece; Which makes her seat of Belmont Colchos' strand, And many Jasons come in quest of her. O my Antonio, had I but the means To hold a rival place with one of them,	**BASSANIO** In Belmont there's a lady who has inherited a lot of money, And she is a beauty and more importantly, Has a wonderful character. Sometimes from the way she looks at me I can tell that she likes me. Her name is Portia – just as rich As Cato's daughter, Brutus' Portia. The whole world knows that she's a great catch; Because sailing in, from every direction Are distinguished suitors, and her beautiful hair Hangs around her face like a golden fleece, Which makes her Belmont estate like Colchos' strond, And her many suitors, pursuing her, like Jasons. Oh my Antonio, if I had enough money To compete with these suitors,

I have a mind presages me such thrift, That I should questionless be fortunate!	I have a strong feeling that I would definitely win her.
ANTONIO Thou know'st that all my fortunes are at sea;	**ANTONIO** You know that all my finance is tied up in my ships' cargo at sea;
Neither have I money nor commodity To raise a present sum: therefore go forth;	And I don't have cash or anything to sell To raise the money you need at the moment; so go ahead,
Try what my credit can in Venice do:	See what credit you can raise in my name throughout Venice;
That shall be rack'd, even to the uttermost, To furnish thee to Belmont, to fair Portia.	Even if it's at the greatest cost, To enable you to go to Belmont, to beautiful Portia.
Go, presently inquire, and so will I, Where money is, and I no question make To have it of my trust or for my sake.	So you go and so will I, to find out, Where we can get the money from; and I will, without question Guarantee the loan for you.
Exeunt	*Exeunt*

Translation of Act 1 Scene 2

ORIGINAL TEXT	MODERN TRANSLATION
Belmont. A room in PORTIA'S house.	**Belmont. A room in PORTIA'S house.**
Enter PORTIA and NERISSA	*Enter PORTIA and NERISSA*
PORTIA By my troth, Nerissa, my little body is aweary of this great world.	**PORTIA** Truthfully, Nerissa, my little body is tired of this big world.
NERISSA You would be, sweet madam, if your miseries were in the same abundance as your good fortunes are: and yet, for aught I see, they are as sick that surfeit with too much as they that starve with nothing. It is no mean happiness therefore, to be seated in the mean: superfluity comes sooner by white hairs, but competency lives longer.	**NERISSA** You would be, sweet lady, if you had as many misfortunes as you do good fortunes; and yet from what I've seen, those who have too much suffer as much as those who have nothing. Therefore happiness is not to be found in over abundance which ages you more quickly, but in having enough to live on, which helps you to live longer.
PORTIA Good sentences and well pronounced.	**PORTIA** Wise words and well said.
NERISSA They would be better, if well followed.	**NERISSA** They'd be better if they were applied.
PORTIA If to do were as easy as to know what were good to do, chapels had been churches and poor men's cottages princes' palaces. It is a good divine that follows his own instructions: I can easier teach twenty what were good to be done, than be one of the twenty to follow mine own teaching. The brain may devise laws for the blood, but a hot temper leaps o'er a cold decree: such a hare is madness the youth, to skip o'er the meshes of good counsel the cripple. But this reasoning is not in the fashion to choose me a husband. O me, the word 'choose!' I may neither choose whom I would nor refuse whom I dislike; so is the will of a living daughter curbed by the will of a dead father. Is it not hard, Nerissa, that I cannot choose one nor refuse none?	**PORTIA** If it was as easy to do good as it is to know what is good to do, then chapels would be churches and poor men's cottages would be princes' palaces. He is a good clergyman who practices what he preaches; it is easier for me to teach twenty others how to do good, than it is for me to be one of the twenty who follows my own teaching. The brain can make rules for the heart, but a hot temper over- rules a cold command; the madness of youth is like a hare, and good advice is like an old cripple trying to catch it with a net. But thinking like this is not the way for me to choose a husband. Oh my, the word 'choose'! I can neither choose who I like nor turn down anyone I dislike; such is the will of a living daughter controlled by the will of her dead father. It is hard, isn't it Nerissa, that I can neither choose nor refuse anyone?
NERISSA Your father was ever virtuous; and holy men at their death have good inspirations: therefore the lottery, that he hath devised in these three chests of gold, silver and lead, whereof who chooses his meaning chooses you, will, no doubt, never be chosen by any rightly but one who shall rightly love. But what warmth is there in your affection towards any of these princely suitors that are already come?	**NERISSA** Your father was a very good man, and religious men, on their death beds, have divine inspiration; therefore the lottery that he's devised with these three boxes of gold, silver and lead – in which whoever solves the riddle wins you – will without doubt, only be chosen correctly by someone you will really love. But do you like any of these princely suitors who have already come?

PORTIA I pray thee, over-name them; and as thou namest them, I will describe them; and, according to my description, level at my affection.	**PORTIA** Please, run through their names; and as you name them, I will describe them; and you can assess the level of my affection by my description of them.
NERISSA First, there is the Neapolitan prince.	**NERISSA** First of all is the Neapolitan prince.
PORTIA Ay, that's a colt indeed, for he doth nothing but talk of his horse; and he makes it a great appropriation to his own good parts, that he can shoe him himself. I am much afeard my lady his mother played false with a smith.	**PORTIA** Ah yes, he's a young stallion indeed, because all he does is talk about his horse; and he thinks a great deal of himself because he can shoe his horse himself; I am very afraid that his mother may have had an affair with a blacksmith.
NERISSA Then there is the County Palatine.	**NERISSA** Then there is the count Palatine.
PORTIA He doth nothing but frown, as who should say 'If you will not have me, choose:' he hears merry tales and smiles not: I fear he will prove the weeping philosopher when he grows old, being so full of unmannerly sadness in his youth. I had rather be married to a death's-head with a bone in his mouth than to either of these. God defend me from these two!	**PORTIA** He does nothing but frown, as if he's saying 'If you don't want me, then just choose someone else.' Even when he hears funny stories he doesn't smile. I am afraid that he'll turn into a melancholy philosopher when he's old, being so full of disrespectful sadness in his youth. I would rather be married to a skull with a bone in its mouth than to either of these. God save me from these two!
NERISSA How say you by the French lord, Monsieur Le Bon?	**NERISSA** What do you think of the French lord, Monsieur Le Bon?
PORTIA God made him, and therefore let him pass for a man. In truth, I know it is a sin to be a mocker: but, he! why, he hath a horse better than the Neapolitan's, a better bad habit of frowning than the Count Palatine; he is every man in no man; if a throstle sing, he falls straight a capering: he will fence with his own shadow: if I should marry him, I should marry twenty husbands. If he would despise me I would forgive him, for if he love me to madness, I shall never requite him.	**PORTIA** God made him and so I suppose he is a man. Honestly, I know it's a sin to mock, but him – he has a better horse than the Neoploitan's, a better bad habit of frowning that the count Palatine; he's so busy competing with other men that he doesn't know who he is himself. If a songbird sings, he's prancing about dancing; he would fence with his own shadow; if I married him, I would be marrying twenty husbands. If he despised me, I would freely forgive him; because if he was madly in love with me, I could never return his love.
NERISSA What say you, then, to Falconbridge, the young baron of England?	**NERISSA** What do you have to say about Falconbridge, the young English baron?
PORTIA You know I say nothing to him, for he understands not me, nor I him: he hath neither Latin, French, nor Italian, and you will come into the court and swear that I have a poor pennyworth in the English. He is a proper man's picture, but, alas, who can	**PORTIA** You know I can't say anything about him, because he can't understand me, and I can't understand him: he speaks neither Latin, French nor Italian and you know full well how little English I can speak. He is good looking and manly; but how can you

converse with a dumb-show? How oddly he is suited! I think he bought his doublet in Italy, his round hose in France, his bonnet in Germany and his behaviour every where.	communicate with mute good looks? How oddly he is dressed! I think he bought his jacket in Italy, his stockings in France, his hat in Germany and his behaviour from everywhere.
NERISSA What think you of the Scottish lord, his neighbour?	**NERISSA** What do you think of his neighbour, the Scottish lord?
PORTIA That he hath a neighbourly charity in him, for he borrowed a box of the ear of the Englishman and swore he would pay him again when he was able: I think the Frenchman became his surety and sealed under for another.	**PORTIA** That he has neighbourly goodwill in him, because he took a slap on the ear from the Englishman, and didn't immediately retaliate but promised to pay him back later; I think the French man became his guarantor and sealed the deal with another slap.
NERISSA How like you the young German, the Duke of Saxony's nephew?	**NERISSA** How do you like the young German, the Duke of Saxony's nephew?
PORTIA Very vilely in the morning, when he is sober, and most vilely in the afternoon, when he is drunk: when he is best, he is a little worse than a man, and when he is worst, he is little better than a beast: and the worst fall that ever fell, I hope I shall make shift to go without him.	**PORTIA** Very disagreeable in the morning when he is sober; and most disagreeable in the afternoon when he is drunk. At best, he's a little less than a man, and at worst, he's a little better than an animal. And if he had a tragic accident, I'm sure I would find a way to go on without him.
NERISSA If he should offer to choose, and choose the right casket, you should refuse to perform your father's will, if you should refuse to accept him.	**NERISSA** If he offers to choose one of the boxes, and he chooses the correct box, you'll be refusing to carry out your father's last wishes, if you refuse to accept him.
PORTIA Therefore, for fear of the worst, I pray thee, set a deep glass of rhenish wine on the contrary casket, for if the devil be within and that temptation without, I know he will choose it. I will do any thing, Nerissa, ere I'll be married to a sponge.	**PORTIA** So, just in case, please put a big glass of German wine on the wrong box; because if even the devil were in the box and the temptation of wine were on top of the box, I know that he'll choose it. I will do anything, Nerissa, rather than ever be married to a drunk.
NERISSA You need not fear, lady, the having any of these lords: they have acquainted me with their determinations; which is, indeed, to return to their home and to trouble you with no more suit, unless you may be won by some other sort than your father's imposition depending on the caskets.	**NERISSA** You don't have to worry, my lady, that you'll have to have any of these lords; they've told me their intentions, which is to go back to their homes and not to bother you by pursuing you any longer, unless you could be won in some other way rather than your father's 'choose the correct box' demand.
PORTIA If I live to be as old as Sibylla, I will die as chaste as Diana, unless I be obtained by the manner of my father's will. I am glad this parcel of wooers are so reasonable, for there is not one among them but I dote on his very absence, and I pray God grant	**PORTIA** If I live to be as old as the very old Sibylla, I will die a virgin like the goddess Diana, unless someone wins me in the way laid down in my father's will. I am glad that this group of wooers are so sensible; because there's not one among them whose

them a fair departure.	absence I won't adore, and I am praying that God will grant them a good journey home.
NERISSA Do you not remember, lady, in your father's time, a Venetian, a scholar and a soldier, that came hither in company of the Marquis of Montferrat?	**NERISSA** Do you remember, my lady, when your father was alive, a Venetian scholar and soldier who accompanied the Marquis of Montferrat here?
PORTIA Yes, yes, it was Bassanio; as I think, he was so called.	**PORTIA** Yes, yes, it was Bassanio; I think that was his name.
NERISSA True, madam: he, of all the men that ever my foolish eyes looked upon, was the best deserving a fair lady.	**NERISSA** That's him, madam; of all the men I've ever set eyes on, he was the most deserving of a beautiful wife.
PORTIA I remember him well, and I remember him worthy of thy praise.	**PORTIA** I remember him well, and he is deserving of your praise.
Enter a Serving-man	*Enter a Serving-man*
How now! what news?	Hello! What news do you bring?
Servant The four strangers seek for you, madam, to take their leave: and there is a forerunner come from a fifth, the Prince of Morocco, who brings word the prince his master will be here to-night.	**SERVANT** The four suitors are looking for you, madam, to wish you farewell; and there is a messenger from a fifth suitor, the Prince of Morocco, who announces that his master the Prince will be here tonight.
PORTIA If I could bid the fifth welcome with so good a heart as I can bid the other four farewell, I should be glad of his approach: if he have the condition of a saint and the complexion of a devil, I had rather he should shrive me than wive me. Come, Nerissa. Sirrah, go before. Whiles we shut the gates upon one wooer, another knocks at the door.	**PORTIA** If I could welcome the fifth suitor with as happy a heart as I am saying farewell to the other four, I would be glad of his arrival; If he is as good as a saint but as dark as the devil, I would rather he listened to my confession than marry me. Come on, Nerissa. Servant, go ahead of us. Just as we're closing the gate on one suitor, another one is knocking at the door.
Exeunt	*Exeunt*

Translation of Act 1 Scene 3

ORIGINAL TEXT	MODERN TRANSLATION
Venice. A public place.	**Venice. A public place.**
Enter BASSANIO and SHYLOCK	*Enter BASSANIO and SHYLOCK*
SHYLOCK Three thousand ducats; well.	**SHYLOCK** Three thousand ducats – hmmm.
BASSANIO Ay, sir, for three months.	**BASSANIO** Yes, sir, for three months.
SHYLOCK For three months; well.	**SHYLOCK** For three months – hmmm.
BASSANIO For the which, as I told you, Antonio shall be bound.	**BASSANIO** As I told you, Antonio shall become guarantor.
SHYLOCK Antonio shall become bound; well.	**SHYLOCK** Antonio shall become guarantor.
BASSANIO May you stead me? will you pleasure me? shall I know your answer?	**BASSANIO** Will you lend me the money? Will you help me? Have you decided?
SHYLOCK Three thousand ducats for three months and Antonio bound.	**SHYLOCK** Three thousand ducats for three months and Antonio as guarantor.
BASSANIO Your answer to that.	**BASSANIO** Your answer.
SHYLOCK Antonio is a good man.	**SHYLOCK** Antonio is a good man.
BASSANIO Have you heard any imputation to the contrary?	**BASSANIO** Have you heard anything to the contrary?
SHYLOCK Oh, no, no, no, no: my meaning in saying he is a good man is to have you understand me that he is sufficient. Yet his means are in supposition: he hath an argosy bound to Tripolis, another to the Indies; I understand moreover, upon the Rialto, he hath a third at Mexico, a fourth for England, and other ventures he hath, squandered abroad. But ships are but boards, sailors but men: there be land-rats and water-rats, water-thieves and land-thieves, I mean pirates, and then there is the peril of waters, winds and rocks. The man is, notwithstanding, sufficient. Three thousand ducats; I think I may take his bond.	**SHYLOCK** Oh, not at all; what I mean when I say that he's a good man Is that you need to understand that although he is honourable; His finances are uncertain: He has a cargo ship sailing to Tripolis, and another one bound for the Indies; I've heard from the business world at the Rialto, He has a third at Mexico, a fourth heading for England – And he has other ventures which he's risked, abroad. But ships are only pieces of wood, sailors just men; there are land-rats and water-rats,

	thieves and robbers – I mean pirates; and then there are the perils of the sea, storms and rocks. In spite of all this, the man's honour is sufficient. Three thousand ducats – I think I can rely on him as guarantor.
BASSANIO Be assured you may.	**BASSANIO** Rest assured, you most certainly can.
SHYLOCK I will be assured I may; and, that I may be assured, I will bethink me. May I speak with Antonio?	**SHYLOCK** I most certainly will be assured; and to make sure of this, I will consider carefully a plan. Can I talk to Antonio?
BASSANIO If it please you to dine with us.	**BASSANIO** You're welcome to have dinner with us.
SHYLOCK Yes, to smell pork; to eat of the habitation which your prophet the Nazarite conjured the devil into. I will buy with you, sell with you, talk with you, walk with you, and so following, but I will not eat with you, drink with you, nor pray with you. What news on the Rialto? Who is he comes here?	**SHYLOCK** Yes, to smell pork, to eat the animal which your prophet, Jesus, sent the devil into! No way! I will buy with you, sell with you, talk with you, walk with you and so on; but I will not eat with you ,drink with you, or pray with you. What's the news in the business arena today? Who's this?
Enter ANTONIO	*Enter ANTONIO*
BASSANIO This is Signior Antonio.	**BASSANIO** This is Mr Antonio.
SHYLOCK [Aside] How like a fawning publican he looks! I hate him for he is a Christian, But more for that in low simplicity He lends out money gratis and brings down The rate of usance here with us in Venice. If I can catch him once upon the hip, I will feed fat the ancient grudge I bear him. He hates our sacred nation, and he rails, Even there where merchants most do congregate, On me, my bargains and my well-won thrift, Which he calls interest. Cursed be my tribe, If I forgive him!	**SHYLOCK** (Aside) He looks just like a bootlicking publican! I hate him because he's a Christian; But even more because, without thinking of the consequences for the rest of us, He lends money, interest free, which lowers The rate of interest we can charge in Venice. If I can get the better of him, just once, I will pay back fully the ancient grudge I have against him. He hates Jews and he constantly protests, In front of all the other gathered merchants, About me, my fair deals, and my hard earned profits, Which he calls interest. I'll be letting my fellow Jews down If I forgive him!
BASSANIO Shylock, do you hear?	**BASSANIO** Shylock, are you listening?
SHYLOCK I am debating of my present store,	**SHYLOCK** I am thinking about how much money I have at the moment,

And, by the near guess of my memory, I cannot instantly raise up the gross Of full three thousand ducats. What of that? Tubal, a wealthy Hebrew of my tribe, Will furnish me. But soft! how many months Do you desire?	And, if I remember rightly, I can't immediately raise the whole three thousand ducats. But what does that matter? Tubal, a wealthy Jewish friend of mine, Will supply me. But be quiet! how many months do you need the money for?
To ANTONIO	*To ANTONIO*
Rest you fair, good signior; Your worship was the last man in our mouths.	Good day to you, good man; We were just singing your praises.
ANTONIO Shylock, although I neither lend nor borrow By taking nor by giving of excess, Yet, to supply the ripe wants of my friend, I'll break a custom. Is he yet possess'd How much ye would?	**ANTONIO** Shylock, even though I don't lend or borrow By charging or paying interest, I will, to help a friend in desperate need, however, Break the habit of a lifetime. (To Bassanio) Does he know yet How much you want to borrow?
SHYLOCK Ay, ay, three thousand ducats.	**SHYLOCK** Yes, yes, three thousand ducats.
ANTONIO And for three months.	**ANTONIO** And for three months.
SHYLOCK I had forgot; three months; you told me so. Well then, your bond; and let me see; but hear you; Methought you said you neither lend nor borrow Upon advantage.	**SHYLOCK** I'd forgotten – three months; you did tell me. Well then, your guarantee; and let me see - but listen, I thought you said that you don't lend or borrow For profit.
ANTONIO I do never use it.	**ANTONIO** I never do business that way.
SHYLOCK When Jacob grazed his uncle Laban's sheep-- This Jacob from our holy Abram was, As his wise mother wrought in his behalf, The third possessor; ay, he was the third--	**SHYLOCK** When Jacob was looking after his uncle Laban's sheep – This Jacob, our holy Abram's grandson became, With his mother's clever help and assistance, The third heir; yes, he became the third –
ANTONIO And what of him? did he take interest?	**ANTONIO** And what about him? Did he take interest?
SHYLOCK No, not take interest, not, as you would say, Directly interest: mark what Jacob did. When Laban and himself were compromised That all the eanlings which were streak'd and pied Should fall as Jacob's hire, the ewes, being rank, In the end of autumn turned to the rams, And, when the work of generation was Between these woolly breeders in the act,	**SHYLOCK** No, he didn't take interest; not, as you would say, Straightforward interest; listen to what Jacob did: When he and Laban came to an agreement That all the lambs which were speckled and spotted Would be Jacob's pay, the ewes, when they were fertile, at the end of autumn mated with the rams; And whilst the process of reproduction was Taking place between these sheep,

The skilful shepherd peel'd me certain wands, And, in the doing of the deed of kind, He stuck them up before the fulsome ewes, Who then conceiving did in eaning time Fall parti-colour'd lambs, and those were Jacob's. This was a way to thrive, and he was blest: And thrift is blessing, if men steal it not.	The clever shepherd peeled the bark off several different types of branches, And whilst they were mating, He positioned the branches in full view of the fertile ewes, Who then conceived and at lambing time Gave birth to speckled and spotted lambs and they were then Jacob's pay. This was a way to prosper and he was blessed; And prosperity is a blessing, if you don't steal to get it.
ANTONIO This was a venture, sir, that Jacob served for; A thing not in his power to bring to pass, But sway'd and fashion'd by the hand of heaven. Was this inserted to make interest good? Or is your gold and silver ewes and rams?	**ANTONIO** This was a business enterprise, sir, that Jacob worked for; It wasn't anything that he did, that caused this to happen, But it was caused and created by the hand of God. Are you telling me this to justify charging interest? Or do you deal in ewes and rams too?
SHYLOCK I cannot tell; I make it breed as fast: But note me, signior.	**SHYLOCK** I can't say; but my money multiplies just as fast. But pay attention, siginor.
ANTONIO Mark you this, Bassanio, The devil can cite Scripture for his purpose. An evil soul producing holy witness Is like a villain with a smiling cheek, A goodly apple rotten at the heart: O, what a goodly outside falsehood hath!	**ANTONO** (ASIDE) Take note of this, Bassanio, The devil can quote scripture for his own benefit. An evil soul misusing Holy scripture Is like a criminal with a false smile, Looks like a good apple but is rotten to the core. O, how genuine on the outside, liars can appear!
SHYLOCK Three thousand ducats; 'tis a good round sum. Three months from twelve; then, let me see; the rate--	**SHYLOCK** Three thousand ducats – it's a good round sum. Three months from twelve; let me see, what the interest rate will be -
ANTONIO Well, Shylock, shall we be beholding to you?	**ANTONIO** Well, Shylock, are you going to lend us the money?
SHYLOCK Signior Antonio, many a time and oft In the Rialto you have rated me About my moneys and my usances: Still have I borne it with a patient shrug, For sufferance is the badge of all our tribe. You call me misbeliever, cut-throat dog, And spit upon my Jewish gaberdine, And all for use of that which is mine own. Well then, it now appears you need my help: Go to, then; you come to me, and you say 'Shylock, we would have moneys:' you say so; You, that did void your rheum upon my beard And foot me as you spurn a stranger cur	**SHYLOCK** Signior Antonio, many times In the Rialto you have criticised me About my finances and business practices; But I have always been patient and just shrugged it off, Because Jews have always endured suffering; You call me a heathen, ruthless dog, And spit on my Jewish coat, And all because of the way I manage my own money. However, it now appears that you need my help; So then; you come to me and you say 'Shylock, we need some money'. You say this – You, who spat on my beard And kick me, like you'd shove a stray mongrel

Over your threshold: moneys is your suit	Out of your front door; you're after money.
What should I say to you? Should I not say	What do you expect me to say to you? I should say
'Hath a dog money? is it possible	' Do dogs have money? How can a mongrel possibly
A cur can lend three thousand ducats?' Or	lend three thousand ducats?'
Shall I bend low and in a bondman's key,	Should I bow before you and like a slave,
With bated breath and whispering humbleness, Say	With a hushed voice humbly answer you,
this;	Saying this:
'Fair sir, you spit on me on Wednesday last;	' Kind sir, you spat on me last Wednesday,
You spurn'd me such a day; another time	You despised me on another day; on another occasion
You call'd me dog; and for these courtesies	You called me a dog; and because of this respectful treatment
I'll lend you thus much moneys'?	I'll lend you that much money'?
ANTONIO	**ANTONIO**
I am as like to call thee so again,	I'm quite likely to call you that again,
To spit on thee again, to spurn thee too.	To spit on you again and to despise you too.
If thou wilt lend this money, lend it not	If you're willing to lend this money, then don't lend it
As to thy friends; for when did friendship take	As if lending to friends – because how could a genuine friend charge
A breed for barren metal of his friend?	Interest on money he's lent to a friend? -
But lend it rather to thine enemy,	But instead lend it to your enemey,
Who, if he break, thou mayst with better face	Who, if he goes back on the agreement, you could more happily
Exact the penalty.	Make pay the penalty.
SHYLOCK	**SHYLOCK**
Why, look you, how you storm!	Well, look at you, in a rage!
I would be friends with you and have your love,	I want to be your friend and you to be mine,
Forget the shames that you have stain'd me with,	To forget the shameful ways you have humiliated me,
Supply your present wants and take no doit	To supply what you want and to make no charge
Of usance for my moneys, and you'll not hear me:	For setting up this loan, and you won't listen to me.
This is kind I offer.	This is a good hearted offer.
BASSANIO	**BASSANIO**
This were kindness.	This really is a good hearted offer.
SHYLOCK	**SHYLOCK**
This kindness will I show.	I will show you my good heart.
Go with me to a notary, seal me there	Come with me to a notary, and you can sign a
Your single bond; and, in a merry sport,	contract and just for fun,
If you repay me not on such a day,	If you don't pay me back on the agreed day,
In such a place, such sum or sums as are	In the agreed place, the agreed amount which is
Express'd in the condition, let the forfeit	Documented on the contract, let the penalty
Be nominated for an equal pound	Be named that a pound in weight
Of your fair flesh, to be cut off and taken	Of your beautiful flesh, is cut off and removed
In what part of your body pleaseth me.	From whatever part of your body I choose.
ANTONIO	**ANTONIO**
Content, i' faith: I'll seal to such a bond	Happy with that deal; I'll agree to that contract,
And say there is much kindness in the Jew.	And even say that there's a good heart inside this Jew.
BASSANIO	**BASSANIO**
You shall not seal to such a bond for me:	You mustn't sign a contract like that for me;

I'll rather dwell in my necessity.	I'd rather go without the money.
ANTONIO Why, fear not, man; I will not forfeit it: Within these two months, that's a month before This bond expires, I do expect return Of thrice three times the value of this bond.	**ANTONIO** Oh, don't worry, man; I won't be paying any penalty; Within the next two months – that's a month before This contract expires – I expect profits Of nine times the value of this loan.
SHYLOCK O father Abram, what these Christians are, Whose own hard dealings teaches them suspect The thoughts of others! Pray you, tell me this; If he should break his day, what should I gain By the exaction of the forfeiture? A pound of man's flesh taken from a man Is not so estimable, profitable neither, As flesh of muttons, beefs, or goats. I say, To buy his favour, I extend this friendship: If he will take it, so; if not, adieu; And, for my love, I pray you wrong me not.	**SHYLOCK** Oh father Abram, what are these Christians like, The way they deal harshly with others causes them to suspect The motives of others! Please answer this: If he passes the deadline, what do I stand to gain By demanding the penalty? A pound of human flesh taken from a man Cannot be valued and it can't be profitable either, Like the flesh of mutton, beef or goats. I am saying this, To get in his good books, to be a friend to him; If he will accept the offer, good; if not, goodbye; And I hope that you don't misjudge my good intentions.
ANTONIO Yes Shylock, I will seal unto this bond.	**ANTONIO** Yes, Shylock, I will sign this contract.
SHYLOCK Then meet me forthwith at the notary's; Give him direction for this merry bond, And I will go and purse the ducats straight, See to my house, left in the fearful guard Of an unthrifty knave, and presently I will be with you.	**SHYLOCK** Then meet me shortly at the notary's; Tell him the details of our amusing contract, And I will go to get the money straight away, Check on my house, which I fearfully left in the care Of a wasteful scoundrel and I'll be with you soon.
ANTONIO Hie thee, gentle Jew. *Exit Shylock* The Hebrew will turn Christian: he grows kind.	**ANTONIO** Hurry up, gentle Jew. *Exit Shylock* The Jew is turning into a Christian: he's becoming so kind.
BASSANIO I like not fair terms and a villain's mind.	**BASSANIO** I don't trust a villain who offers good deals.
ANTONIO Come on: in this there can be no dismay; My ships come home a month before the day.	**ANTONIO** Come on; nothing can go wrong; My ships will be home a month before the contract expires.
Exeunt	*Exeunt*

Translation of Act 2 Scene 1

ORIGINAL TEXT	MODERN TRANSLATION
Belmont. A room in PORTIA'S house.	**Belmont. A room in PORTIA'S house.**
Flourish of cornets. Enter the PRINCE OF MOROCCO and his train; PORTIA, NERISSA, and others attending	*Flourish of cornets. Enter the PRINCE OF MOROCCO and his train; PORTIA, NERISSA, and others attending*
MOROCCO	**MOROCCO**
Mislike me not for my complexion,	Don't reject me because of my skin colour,
The shadow'd livery of the burnish'd sun,	It is caused by the hot sunshine,
To whom I am a neighbour and near bred.	In the country where I was born.
Bring me the fairest creature northward born,	Bring to me the most handsome suitor from the north,
Where Phoebus' fire scarce thaws the icicles,	Where the sun's burning rays would barely melt the icicles,
And let us make incision for your love,	And let us compete for your love by cutting ourselves
To prove whose blood is reddest, his or mine.	To prove whose blood is the reddest, his or mine.
I tell thee, lady, this aspect of mine	I assure you, lady, that my skin colour
Hath fear'd the valiant: by my love I swear	Has made even the fearless fear me; I swear, by my love for you that
The best-regarded virgins of our clime	The most sought after virgins from my country
Have loved it too: I would not change this hue,	Have loved my skin colour too. I would not change this complexion,
Except to steal your thoughts, my gentle queen.	Unless it was to draw your attention, my gentle queen.
PORTIA	**PORTIA**
In terms of choice I am not solely led	When choosing, I am not led only
By nice direction of a maiden's eyes;	By what I find attractive in a suitor's looks;
Besides, the lottery of my destiny	Anyway, the outcome of my destiny
Bars me the right of voluntary choosing:	Doesn't allow me the right to choose for myself.
But if my father had not scanted me	But, if my father had not cut off my right to choose,
And hedged me by his wit, to yield myself	And , in his wisdom, limited me to giving myself
His wife who wins me by that means I told you,	As wife to the one who wins me by the way I have explained to you,
Yourself, renowned prince, then stood as fair	Then you, distinguished prince, would have been as attractive to me
As any comer I have look'd on yet	As any other suitor I have met so far
For my affection.	Competing to marry me.
MOROCCO	**MOROCCO**
Even for that I thank you:	Thank you for saying that.
Therefore, I pray you, lead me to the caskets	So, please, take me to the boxes
To try my fortune. By this scimitar	To try my luck. I swear by this sword,
That slew the Sophy and a Persian prince	Which killed the King of Persia and a Persian prince,
That won three fields of Sultan Solyman,	That won three battles with Sultan Solyman,
I would outstare the sternest eyes that look,	I would face the fiercest foe,
Outbrave the heart most daring on the earth,	Be braver than the bravest heart on earth,
Pluck the young sucking cubs from the she-bear,	Steal young suckling cubs away from their fierce mother bear,

Yea, mock the lion when he roars for prey,	Even, torment a lion when he's hungry and roaring for food,
To win thee, lady. But, alas the while! If Hercules and Lichas play at dice Which is the better man, the greater throw	To have you as mine, lady. But this is unfair! If Hercules and his servant Lichas played dice It wouldn't matter which was the stronger man, the better roll of the dice
May turn by fortune from the weaker hand: So is Alcides beaten by his page;	May, just by chance, be thrown by the weaker man. In just the same way Alcides could be beaten by his servant;
And so may I, blind fortune leading me, Miss that which one unworthier may attain, And die with grieving.	And so could I, by sheer bad luck, Lose you to an unworthier suitor, And die of grief.
PORTIA You must take your chance, And either not attempt to choose at all	**PORTIA** You have to take your chances, And choose to not even try to pick the correct box at all,
Or swear before you choose, if you choose wrong	Or swear before you choose, that if you pick the wrong box,
Never to speak to lady afterward In way of marriage: therefore be advised.	You'll never propose to any woman afterwards Asking her to marry you; so now you know that it is an important decision.
MOROCCO Nor will not. Come, bring me unto my chance.	**MOROCCO** I won't propose to anyone else; take me to where I will try my luck.
PORTIA First, forward to the temple: after dinner Your hazard shall be made.	**PORTIA** Let's go to the temple first. After dinner Your fate will be sealed.
MOROCCO Good fortune then! To make me blest or cursed'st among men.	**MOROCCO** I will try my luck then, And will become the luckiest or unluckiest man in the world!
Cornets, and exeunt	*Cornets, and exeunt*

Translation of Act 2 Scene 2

ORIGINAL TEXT	MODERN TRANSLATION
SCENE II. Venice. A street.	**Venice. A street.**
Enter LAUNCELOT	*Enter LAUNCELOT*
LAUNCELOT Certainly my conscience will serve me to run from this Jew my master. The fiend is at mine elbow and tempts me saying to me 'Gobbo, Launcelot Gobbo, good Launcelot,' or 'good Gobbo,' or good Launcelot Gobbo, use your legs, take the start, run away. My conscience says 'No; take heed,' honest Launcelot; take heed, honest Gobbo, or, as aforesaid, 'honest Launcelot Gobbo; do not run; scorn running with thy heels.' Well, the most courageous fiend bids me pack: 'Via!' says the fiend; 'away!' says the fiend; 'for the heavens, rouse up a brave mind,' says the fiend, 'and run.' Well, my conscience, hanging about the neck of my heart, says very wisely to me 'My honest friend Launcelot, being an honest man's son,' or rather an honest woman's son; for, indeed, my father did something smack, something grow to, he had a kind of taste; well, my conscience says 'Launcelot, budge not.' 'Budge,' says the fiend. 'Budge not,' says my conscience. 'Conscience,' say I, 'you counsel well;' ' Fiend,' say I, 'you counsel well:' to be ruled by my conscience, I should stay with the Jew my master, who, God bless the mark, is a kind of devil; and, to run away from the Jew, I should be ruled by the fiend, who, saving your reverence, is the devil himself. Certainly the Jew is the very devil incarnal; and, in my conscience, my conscience is but a kind of hard conscience, to offer to counsel me to stay with the Jew. The fiend gives the more friendly counsel: I will run, fiend; my heels are at your command; I will run.	**LAUNCELOT** Surely my conscience will allow me to run away from this Jew my master. The devil is at my elbow tempting me, saying to me 'Gobbo, Launcelot Gobbo, good Launcelot' or 'good Gobbo' or 'good Launcelot Gobbo, use your legs, get going, run away'. My conscience says ' No; listen, honest Launcelot, pay attention, honest Gobbo' or,' honest Launcelot Gobbo, do not run away; refuse outright to run off'. Well, the most courageous devil is ordering me to go. 'Off with you!' says the devil; ' get going!' says the devil. ' For heavens sake, gather all your courage' says the devil 'and run away'. Well, my conscience, weighing me down, says very wisely to me ' My honest friend Launcelot, as you are an honest man's son' or rather ' an honest woman's son'; because my father did have a tendency, was drawn towards, did have a weakness for women- well my conscience says 'Launcelot, don't budge'. ' Run away' says the devil. 'Stay put' says my conscience. 'Conscience,' I say ' your advice is good'. ' Devil,' I say ' your advice is good'. If I let my conscience decide, I would stay with the Jew my master, who – God forgive me! – is a kind of devil; and if were to run away from the Jew, I would be taking the advice of the devil, who –please forgive me Reverend! – is the devil himself. However the Jew is the devil incarnate; and my conscience advises me to make the harder choice if I were to choose to stay with the Jew. The devil offers me the easier choice. I will run away, devil; I'm following your command; I'm going to run away.
Enter Old GOBBO, with a basket	*Enter Old GOBBO, with a basket*
GOBBO Master young man, you, I pray you, which is the way to master Jew's?	**GOBBO** Young man, excuse me, which way do I go to get to the Jew's house?
LAUNCELOT [Aside] O heavens, this is my true-begotten father! who, being more than sand-blind, high-gravel blind,	**LAUNCELOT** (Aside) Good heavens! This is my father, who, because he's more than half blind, three quarters

knows me not: I will try confusions with him.	blind, doesn't recognise me. I'll try to play a trick on him.
GOBBO Master young gentleman, I pray you, which is the way to master Jew's?	**GOBBO** Young gentleman, excuse me, which way do I go to get to the Jew's house?
LAUNCELOT Turn up on your right hand at the next turning, but, at the next turning of all, on your left; marry, at the very next turning, turn of no hand, but turn down indirectly to the Jew's house.	**LAUNCELOT** Go right at the next turning, but, at the following turning, go left; at the next crossroads, don't go right or left, but turn down the side road to the Jew's house.
GOBBO By God's sonties, 'twill be a hard way to hit. Can you tell me whether one Launcelot, that dwells with him, dwell with him or no?	**GOBBO** By God's saints, it will be hard to find! Do you know whether a Launcelot is still living there with him?
LAUNCELOT Talk you of young Master Launcelot?	**LAUNCELOT** Do you mean young Master Launcelot?
Aside	*Aside*
Mark me now; now will I raise the waters. Talk you of young Master Launcelot?	Watch this now; now I will get him into deep water. - Do you mean young Master Launcelot?
GOBBO No master, sir, but a poor man's son: his father, though I say it, is an honest exceeding poor man and, God be thanked, well to live.	**GOBBO** Not a master, sir, but the son of a poor man; his father, if I say so myself, is an honest but very poor man, and, thanks be to God, alive and well
LAUNCELOT Well, let his father be what a' will, we talk of young Master Launcelot.	**LAUNCELOT** Well, whatever his father is, we're talking about young Master Launcelot.
GOBBO Your worship's friend and Launcelot, sir.	**GOBBO** Your friend and plain Launcelot, sir.
LAUNCELOT But I pray you, ergo, old man, ergo, I beseech you, talk you of young Master Launcelot?	**LAUNCELOT** But please, I'm asking you, if that's the case, old man, if that is so, I'm seriously asking you, do you mean young Master Launcelot?
GOBBO Of Launcelot, an't please your mastership.	**GOBBO** I'm talking about Launcelot, sir.
LAUNCELOT Ergo, Master Launcelot. Talk not of Master Launcelot, father; for the young gentleman, according to Fates and Destinies and such odd sayings, the Sisters Three and such branches of learning, is indeed deceased, or, as you would say in plain terms, gone to heaven.	**LAUNCELOT** Therefore, you mean Master Launcelot. Don't talk about Master Launcelot, father; for the young gentleman, succumbing to Fate and the Three Goddess Sisters who control destiny and similar belief systems, has died; or, as you would put it, gone to heaven.
GOBBO Marry, God forbid! the boy was the very staff of my age, my very prop.	**GOBBO** Oh, God forbid! The boy was going to be my support in my old age, someone to lean on.

LAUNCELOT Do I look like a cudgel or a hovel-post, a staff or a prop? Do you know me, father?	**LAUNCELOT** Do I look like a make- shift walking stick/ weapon, a crutch or a crook? Do you recognise me, father?
GOBBO Alack the day, I know you not, young gentleman: but, I pray you, tell me, is my boy, God rest his soul, alive or dead?	**GOBBO** Oh heavens above, I don't know who you are, young gentleman; but please tell me, is my boy - God rest his soul! – alive or dead?
LAUNCELOT Do you not know me, father?	**LAUNCELOT** Don't you recognise me, father?
GOBBO Alack, sir, I am sand-blind; I know you not.	**GOBBO** Oh heavens above, sir, I am half blind; I don't recognise you.
LAUNCELOT Nay, indeed, if you had your eyes, you might fail of the knowing me: it is a wise father that knows his own child. Well, old man, I will tell you news of your son: give me your blessing: truth will come to light; murder cannot be hid long; a man's son may, but at the length truth will out.	**LAUNCELOT** No, even if you had perfect eyesight, you may fail to recognise me: it takes a wise father to know his own child. Well, old man, I will tell you news of your son. Give me your blessing; the truth will come to light; murder cannot be hidden for long; a man's son may hide, but in the end, truth will always come out.
GOBBO Pray you, sir, stand up: I am sure you are not Launcelot, my boy.	**GOBBO** Please sir, stand up; I am sure you're not Launcelot my boy.
LAUNCELOT Pray you, let's have no more fooling about it, but give me your blessing: I am Launcelot, your boy that was, your son that is, your child that shall be.	**LAUNCELOT** Please, let's stop joking about it, but give me your blessing; I am Launcelot, who was your boy, who is your son, and who will always be your child.
GOBBO I cannot think you are my son.	**GOBBO** I can't believe that you're my son.
LAUNCELOT I know not what I shall think of that: but I am Launcelot, the Jew's man, and I am sure Margery your wife is my mother.	**LAUNCELOT** I don't know what to think of that; but I am Launcelot, the Jew's servant, and I am sure that Margery, your wife is my mother.
GOBBO Her name is Margery, indeed: I'll be sworn, if thou be Launcelot, thou art mine own flesh and blood. Lord worshipped might he be! what a beard hast thou got! thou hast got more hair on thy chin than Dobbin my fill-horse has on his tail.	**GOBBO** Her name is indeed Margery. I'll swear on the Bible, if you are Launcelot, you are my own flesh and blood. May the Lord be praised, what a long beard you have! You have more hair on your chin than Dobbin my shaft- horse has on his tail.
LAUNCELOT It should seem, then, that Dobbin's tail grows backward: I am sure he had more hair of his tail than I have of my face when I last saw him.	**LAUNCELOT** It would appear then, that Dobbin's tail is growing backwards; I am sure that he had more hair on his tail than I have on my face when I last saw him.

GOBBO Lord, how art thou changed! How dost thou and thy master agree? I have brought him a present. How 'gree you now?	**GOBBO** Lord, you've changed so much! How do you and your master get on? I have brought him a present. How are you?
LAUNCELOT Well, well: but, for mine own part, as I have set up my rest to run away, so I will not rest till I have run some ground. My master's a very Jew: give him a present! give him a halter: I am famished in his service; you may tell every finger I have with my ribs. Father, I am glad you are come: give me your present to one Master Bassanio, who, indeed, gives rare new liveries: if I serve not him, I will run as far as God has any ground. O rare fortune! here comes the man: to him, father; for I am a Jew, if I serve the Jew any longer.	**LAUNCELOT** I'm well, I'm well; but I have made up my mind to run away, so I will not rest until I have put some distance between us. My master's a total Jew. Give him a present! Give him a noose. I am starving working for him; you can count all my ribs. Father, I am glad you have come; give me your present to give to Master Bassanio, who gives his servants beautiful new uniforms; if I can't work for him, then I'll run away to the ends of the earth. Oh what good fortune! Here he comes now. Let's go and talk to him father, because if I work for the Jew any longer I'll become a Jew myself.
Enter BASSANIO, with LEONARDO and other followers	*Enter BASSANIO, with LEONARDO and other followers*
BASSANIO You may do so; but let it be so hasted that supper be ready at the farthest by five of the clock. See these letters delivered; put the liveries to making, and desire Gratiano to come anon to my lodging.	**BASSANIO** That's fine, go ahead; but be quick so that supper is ready by five o'clock at the latest. Make sure these letters are delivered, get the uniforms made, and ask Gratiano to come and visit me soon.
Exit a Servant	*Exit a Servant*
LAUNCELOT To him, father.	**LAUNCELOT** Talk to him, father.
GOBBO God bless your worship!	**GOBBO** (TO BASSANIO) God bless you sir!
BASSANIO Gramercy! wouldst thou aught with me?	**BASSANIO** Many thanks; do you want something?
GOBBO Here's my son, sir, a poor boy,--	**GOBBO** This is my son, sir, a poor boy –
LAUNCELOT Not a poor boy, sir, but the rich Jew's man; that would, sir, as my father shall specify--	**LAUNCELOT** Not a poor boy, sir, but the rich Jew's servant, who would like, sir, as my father will explain –
GOBBO He hath a great infection, sir, as one would say, to serve--	**GOBBO** He would very much like, sir, as one might say, to work for -
LAUNCELOT Indeed, the short and the long is, I serve the Jew, and have a desire, as my father shall specify--	**LAUNCELOT** To cut a long story short, I work for the Jew, and would very much like, as my father will explain
GOBBO His master and he, saving your worship's reverence, are scarce cater-cousins--	**GOBBO** His master and he, with all due respect, could not be described as close friends –

LAUNCELOT To be brief, the very truth is that the Jew, having done me wrong, doth cause me, as my father, being, I hope, an old man, shall frutify unto you--	**LAUNCELOT** In brief, the absolute truth is that the Jew, having wronged me, has forced me, as my father, an old man, will confirm to you -
GOBBO I have here a dish of doves that I would bestow upon your worship, and my suit is--	**GOBBO** I have a gift which I would like to honour you with; and my request is –
LAUNCELOT In very brief, the suit is impertinent to myself, as your worship shall know by this honest old man; and, though I say it, though old man, yet poor man, my father.	**LAUNCELOT** In short, the request is about me, as your worship will find out from this honest old man; and if I say so myself, although this man is old and poor, he is my father.
BASSANIO One speak for both. What would you?	**BASSANIO** Just one of you should speak. What do you want?
LAUNCELOT Serve you, sir.	**LAUNCELOT** Work for you, sir.
GOBBO That is the very defect of the matter, sir.	**GOBBO** That is the fact of the matter, sir.
BASSANIO I know thee well; thou hast obtain'd thy suit: Shylock thy master spoke with me this day, And hath preferr'd thee, if it be preferment To leave a rich Jew's service, to become The follower of so poor a gentleman.	**BASSANIO** I know you well; your request has been granted. Shylock your master spoke to me today, And has recommended you, if it can be recommended To quit working for a rich Jew, to become The employee of such a poor gentleman.
LAUNCELOT The old proverb is very well parted between my master Shylock and you, sir: you have the grace of God, sir, and he hath enough.	**LAUNCELOT** The old proverb 'The Grace of God is Enough' could easily be shared between my master Shylock and you sir: you have the 'Grace of God', sir and he has 'Enough'.
BASSANIO Thou speak'st it well. Go, father, with thy son. Take leave of thy old master and inquire My lodging out. Give him a livery More guarded than his fellows': see it done.	**BASSANIO** Well said. Father, go with your son. Leave your old master, and find out How to get to my home.(To a servant) Give him a uniform More smart than his fellow servants'; make sure it's done.
LAUNCELOT Father, in. I cannot get a service, no; I have ne'er a tongue in my head. Well, if any man in Italy have a fairer table which doth offer to swear upon a book, I shall have good fortune. Go to, here's a simple line of life: here's a small trifle of wives: alas, fifteen wives is nothing! eleven widows and nine maids is a simple coming-in for one man: and then to 'scape drowning thrice, and to be	**LAUNCELOT** Father, let's go. I can't get a job, no! I've never been able to speak! (Looking at his palm) Well, I doubt that any man in Italy has a better palm with which to swear upon a Bible – I have good luck. Here's my life line; here's the small matter of wives; alas fifteen wives is nothing; eleven widows and nine maids is a small start for a man. And then I'll escape drowning three times, and be in great danger when caught in

in peril of my life with the edge of a feather-bed; here are simple scapes. Well, if Fortune be a woman, she's a good wench for this gear. Father, come; I'll take my leave of the Jew in the twinkling of an eye.	bed with another man's wife – but here you can see the lines which are escape routes. Well, if Luck is a lady, she's a good woman for this business. Father, come on; I'll leave that Jew in a twinkling of an eye.
Exeunt Launcelot and Old Gobbo	*Exeunt Launcelot and Old Gobbo*
BASSANIO I pray thee, good Leonardo, think on this: These things being bought and orderly bestow'd, Return in haste, for I do feast to-night My best-esteem'd acquaintance: hie thee, go.	**BASSANIO** Please, good Leonardo, make this a priority. After you've bought these items and presented them to the recipient, Come back quickly, because I am having dinner this evening With someone I greatly respect; go quickly, go.
LEONARDO My best endeavours shall be done herein.	**LENOARDO** Well then, I shall do my very best.
Enter GRATIANO	*Enter GRATIANO*
GRATIANO Where is your master?	**GRATIANO** Where's your master?
LEONARDO Yonder, sir, he walks.	**LEONARDO** He is walking over there, sir.
Exit	*EXIT*
GRATIANO Signior Bassanio!	**GRATIANO** Signior Bassanio!
BASSANIO Gratiano!	**BASSANIO** Gratiano!
GRATIANO I have a suit to you.	**GRATIANO** I have a request to make.
BASSANIO You have obtain'd it.	**BASSANIO** The answer is yes.
GRATIANO You must not deny me: I must go with you to Belmont.	**GRATIANO** Please don't say no: I really want to go with you to Belmont.
BASSANIO Why then you must. But hear thee, Gratiano; T hou art too wild, too rude and bold of voice; Parts that become thee happily enough And in such eyes as ours appear not faults; But where thou art not known, why, there they show Something too liberal. Pray thee, take pain To allay with some cold drops of modesty Thy skipping spirit, lest through thy wild behavior I be misconstrued in the place I go to,	**BASSANIO** Well then, you can accompany me. But listen, Gratiano: You are too wild, too rude and loud – These ways suit you well enough, And in our eyes there's nothing wrong with that; But to people who don't know you, well, they appear A bit too wild. Please take great care To tone down with a bit of common sense Your high spirits; otherwise through your wild behaviour

And lose my hopes.	I may be misunderstood in the place where I am going And lose my hope of winning Portia.
GRATIANO Signior Bassanio, hear me: If I do not put on a sober habit, Talk with respect and swear but now and then, Wear prayer-books in my pocket, look demurely, Nay more, while grace is saying, hood mine eyes Thus with my hat, and sigh and say 'amen,' Use all the observance of civility, Like one well studied in a sad ostent To please his grandam, never trust me more.	**GRATIANO** Signior Bassanio, listen to me: If I don't dress respectfully, Talk respectfully and swear only occasionally, Carry prayer- books in my pockets, appear solemn, And even more, while grace is being said, close my eyes Remove my hat and sigh, and say 'amen'. Be on my very best behaviour Like someone who is used to having to appear well behaved To please his grandma, then never trust me again.
BASSANIO Well, we shall see your bearing.	**BASSANIO** Well, we'll see how you conduct yourself.
GRATIANO Nay, but I bar to-night: you shall not gauge me By what we do to-night.	**GRATIANO** OK, but not tonight; you can't assess me By how we conduct ourselves tonight.
BASSANIO No, that were pity: I would entreat you rather to put on Your boldest suit of mirth, for we have friends That purpose merriment. But fare you well: I have some business.	**BASSANIO** No, that would be a pity; I would rather encourage you to put on Your most outrageous sense of humour, because our friends Are determined to have fun. But goodbye for now; I have to attend to some business.
GRATIANO And I must to Lorenzo and the rest: But we will visit you at supper-time.	**GRATIANO** And I have to meet up with Lorenzo and the others; But we will see you at suppertime.
Exeunt	*Exeunt*

Translation of Act 2 Scene 3

ORIGINAL TEXT	MODERN TRANSLATION
The same. A room in SHYLOCK'S house.	**The same. A room in SHYLOCK'S house.**
Enter JESSICA and LAUNCELOT	*Enter JESSICA and LAUNCELOT*
JESSICA I am sorry thou wilt leave my father so: Our house is hell, and thou, a merry devil, Didst rob it of some taste of tediousness. But fare thee well, there is a ducat for thee: And, Launcelot, soon at supper shalt thou see Lorenzo, who is thy new master's guest: Give him this letter; do it secretly; And so farewell: I would not have my father See me in talk with thee.	**JESSICA** I'm sorry that you're leaving my father like this. Our house is like hell; and you, funny devil, Alleviated the monotony. But goodbye; here is a gold coin for you; And, Launcelot, soon at supper you will see Lorenzo, who is your new master's guest. Give him this letter; do it secretly. And so goodbye. I don't want my father To see me talking to you.
LAUNCELOT Adieu! tears exhibit my tongue. Most beautiful pagan, most sweet Jew! if a Christian did not play the knave and get thee, I am much deceived. But, adieu: these foolish drops do something drown my manly spirit: adieu.	**LAUNCELOT** Goodbye! My tears show what I want to say. Most beautiful pagan, most sweet Jew! If a Christian doesn't use dishonesty to get you, I'll be very surprised. But goodbye! These foolish tears make me appear unmanly; adieu!
JESSICA Farewell, good Launcelot.	**JESSICA** Goodbye, good Launcelot.
Exit Launcelot	*Exit Launcelot*
Alack, what heinous sin is it in me To be ashamed to be my father's child! But though I am a daughter to his blood, I am not to his manners. O Lorenzo, If thou keep promise, I shall end this strife, Become a Christian and thy loving wife.	Oh dear, what a terrible sin it is for me To be ashamed to be my father's child! But though I am his daughter by blood, I am not by behaviour. Oh Lorenzo, If you keep your promise, I will end this hostility, And become a Christian and your loving wife.
Exit	*Exit*

Translation of Act 2 Scene 4

ORIGINAL TEXT	MODERN TRANSLATION
The same. A street.	**The same. A street.**
Enter GRATIANO, LORENZO, SALARINO, and SALANIO	*Enter GRATIANO, LORENZO, SALARINO, and SALANIO*
LORENZO Nay, we will slink away in supper-time, Disguise us at my lodging and return, All in an hour.	**LORENZO** No, we'll sneak away at suppertime, Disguise ourselves at my house, and return, All within an hour.
GRATIANO We have not made good preparation.	**GRATIANO** We're not well prepared.
SALARINO We have not spoke us yet of torchbearers.	**SALARINO** We haven't yet discussed who'll be torch -bearers.
SALANIO 'Tis vile, unless it may be quaintly order'd, And better in my mind not undertook.	**SOLANIO** It's not worthwhile, unless it's beautifully organised; And in my opinion, best not undertaken.
LORENZO 'Tis now but four o'clock: we have two hours To furnish us.	**LORENZO** It's only four o'clock now; we have two hours To get ready.
Enter LAUNCELOT, with a letter	*Enter LAUNCELOT, with a letter*
Friend Launcelot, what's the news?	Launcelot, my friend, what's the news?
LAUNCELOT An it shall please you to break up this, it shall seem to signify.	**LAUNCELOT** If you'd like to open this letter, it will be revealed.
LORENZO I know the hand: in faith, 'tis a fair hand; And whiter than the paper it writ on Is the fair hand that writ.	**LORENZO** I know this hand writing; I believe, it is beautiful handwriting, And whiter than the paper it wrote on Is the beautiful hand that wrote it.
GRATIANO Love-news, in faith.	**GRATIANO** A love letter, I believe.
LAUNCELOT By your leave, sir.	**LAUNCELOT** With your permission, sir I will leave.
LORENZO Whither goest thou?	**LORENZO** Where are you going?
LAUNCELOT Marry, sir, to bid my old master the Jew to sup to-night with my new master the Christian.	**LAUNCELOT** Well, sir, to ask my old master, the Jew, to dine tonight with my new master, the Christian.

LORENZO Hold here, take this: tell gentle Jessica I will not fail her; speak it privately. Go, gentlemen,	**LORENZO** Wait a minute, take this. Tell gentle Jessica I won't let her down; tell her in private. Go, gentlemen,
Exit Launcelot	*Exit Launcelot*
Will you prepare you for this masque tonight?	Will you get ready now for the masquerade ball tonight?
I am provided of a torch-bearer.	I've been given a torch bearer.
SALAriNIO Ay, marry, I'll be gone about it straight.	**SALARINO** Yes, definitely, I'll get started straight away.
SALANIO And so will I.	**SOLANIO** Me too.
LORENZO Meet me and Gratiano At Gratiano's lodging some hour hence.	**LORENZO** Meet me and Gratiano At Gratiano's lodging about an hour from now.
SALARINO 'Tis good we do so.	**SALARINO** It'll be good to do that.
Exeunt SALARINO and SALANIO	*Exeunt SALARINO and SALANIO*
GRATIANO Was not that letter from fair Jessica?	**GRATIANO** Wasn't that letter from beautiful Jessica?
LORENZO I must needs tell thee all. She hath directed How I shall take her from her father's house, What gold and jewels she is furnish'd with, What page's suit she hath in readiness. If e'er the Jew her father come to heaven, It will be for his gentle daughter's sake: And never dare misfortune cross her foot, Unless she do it under this excuse, That she is issue to a faithless Jew. Come, go with me; peruse this as thou goest:	**LORENZO** I have to tell you everything. She has explained How I will take her from her father's house; What gold and jewels she has with her; What page's suit she has ready to wear. If ever the Jew her father gets into heaven, It will be because of his gentle daughter's goodness; And bad luck will never cross her path, Unless it's for this reason, That she's the daughter of a faithless Jew. Come on, let's go, read through this letter on the way;
Fair Jessica shall be my torch-bearer.	Beautiful Jessica will be my torch bearer.
Exeunt	*Exeunt*

Translation of Act 2 Scene 5

ORIGINAL TEXT	MODERN TRANSLATION
The same. Before SHYLOCK'S house.	**The same. Before SHYLOCK'S house.**
Enter SHYLOCK and LAUNCELOT	*Enter SHYLOCK and LAUNCELOT*
SHYLOCK Well, thou shalt see, thy eyes shall be thy judge, The difference of old Shylock and Bassanio:-- What, Jessica!--thou shalt not gormandise, As thou hast done with me:--What, Jessica!-- And sleep and snore, and rend apparel out;-- Why, Jessica, I say!	**SHYLOCK** Well, you'll see; I'll let you be the judge, Of the difference between old Shylock and Bassanio.- Jessica! - You won't be gorging yourself on fine food As you have done, working for me - Jessica! - And sleep and snore, and wear your clothes out – Jessica, I'm calling you!
LAUNCELOT Why, Jessica!	**LAUNCELOT** Jessica!
SHYLOCK Who bids thee call? I do not bid thee call.	**SHYLOCK** Who told you to call her? I'm not telling you to call her.
LAUNCELOT Your worship was wont to tell me that I could do nothing without bidding.	**LAUNCELOT** It was your rule that I could never do anything without your permission.
Enter Jessica	*Enter Jessica*
JESSICA Call you? what is your will?	**JESSICA** Are you calling me? What did you want?
SHYLOCK I am bid forth to supper, Jessica: There are my keys. But wherefore should I go? I am not bid for love; they flatter me: But yet I'll go in hate, to feed upon The prodigal Christian. Jessica, my girl, Look to my house. I am right loath to go: There is some ill a-brewing towards my rest, For I did dream of money-bags to-night.	**SHYLOCK** I am invited to supper, Jessica; Here are my keys. But why should I go? I'm not invited because they love me; they're just flattering me; However, I will go in hate, to fill my belly with the reckless Christian. Jessica, my girl, Look after my house. I really don't want to go; There is something bad and unsettling brewing at the moment, Because I dreamt about money-bags last night.
LAUNCELOT I beseech you, sir, go: my young master doth expect your reproach.	**LAUNCELOT** I beg you to go, sir; my young master is expecting your approach.
SHYLOCK So do I his.	**SHYLOCK** Yes, and I'm expecting his reproach.
LAUNCELOT An they have conspired together, I will not say you shall see a masque; but if you do, then it was not	**LAUNCELOT** They've been plotting together; I'm not predicting a masquerade party, but if there is one, it must have

for nothing that my nose fell a-bleeding on Black-Monday last at six o'clock i' the morning, falling out that year on Ash-Wednesday was four year, in the afternoon.	been a sign when I had that nose bleed on the last Black Monday at six o'clock in the morning, four years after I had a nose bleed on the Ash Wednesday, in the afternoon.
SHYLOCK What, are there masques? Hear you me, Jessica: Lock up my doors; and when you hear the drum And the vile squealing of the wry-neck'd fife, Clamber not you up to the casements then, Nor thrust your head into the public street To gaze on Christian fools with varnish'd faces, But stop my house's ears, I mean my casements: Let not the sound of shallow foppery enter My sober house. By Jacob's staff, I swear, I have no mind of feasting forth to-night: But I will go. Go you before me, sirrah; Say I will come.	**SHYLOCK** What, are there masques? Listen to me Jessica: Lock all the doors, and when you hear the drum, And the dreadful squealing of the shrill, stiff necked flute, Don't climb up to the windows, Or stick your head out into the public street To watch Christian fools with painted faces; But block up my house's ears – I mean the windows; Don't let the sound of shallow stupidity enter My serious house. I swear, on Jacob's staff That I have no desire to go out to dinner tonight; But I will go anyway. Go ahead of me, servant; Tell them I'm coming.
LAUNCELOT I will go before, sir. Mistress, look out at window, for all this, There will come a Christian boy, will be worth a Jewess' eye. *Exit*	**LAUNCELOT** I will go ahead of you, sir. Mistress, when you look out of the window, be on watch for this. There will be a Christian passing by Who deserves to catch a Jewess' eye. *Exit*
SHYLOCK What says that fool of Hagar's offspring, ha?	**SHYLOCK** What's that illegitimate fool saying?
JESSICA His words were 'Farewell mistress;' nothing else.	**JESSICA** He said ' Goodbye mistress'; that's all.
SHYLOCK The patch is kind enough, but a huge feeder; Snail-slow in profit, and he sleeps by day More than the wild-cat: drones hive not with me; Therefore I part with him, and part with him To one that would have him help to waste His borrow'd purse. Well, Jessica, go in; Perhaps I will return immediately: Do as I bid you; shut doors after you: Fast bind, fast find; A proverb never stale in thrifty mind. *Exit*	**SHYLOCK** The fool is kind enough, but eats so much food, Works at a snail's pace, and sleeps in the daytime More than a wild cat; I only keep worker bees in my hive, So I'm letting him go; and letting him go To someone that I'm happy that he'll help to waste The money he's borrowed from me. Jessica, go indoors; I may come back straight away. Do as I told you, shut the doors after you. Keep things locked away safely, you'll find them safe A proverb used frequently by careful people. *Exit*
JESSICA Farewell; and if my fortune be not crost, I have a father, you a daughter, lost. *Exit*	**JESSICA** Goodbye; and if luck is with me, I'll lose a father and you'll lose a daughter. *Exit*

Translation of Act 2 Scene 6

ORIGINAL TEXT	MODERN TRANSLATION
The same.	**The same.**
Enter GRATIANO and SALARINO, masqued	*Enter GRATIANO and SALARINO, masqued*
GRATIANO This is the pent-house under which Lorenzo Desired us to make stand.	**GRATIANO** This is the shelter under which Lorenzo Wanted us to wait for him.
SALARINO His hour is almost past.	**SALARINO** He is late.
GRATIANO And it is marvel he out-dwells his hour, For lovers ever run before the clock.	**GRATIANO** And it is surprising that he's late, Because lovers are always early.
SALARINO O, ten times faster Venus' pigeons fly To seal love's bonds new-made, than they are wont To keep obliged faith unforfeited!	**SALARINO** Oh, time flies ten times faster When you're first in love, than it tends to When you've been married for a long time!
GRATIANO That ever holds: who riseth from a feast With that keen appetite that he sits down? Where is the horse that doth untread again His tedious measures with the unbated fire That he did pace them first? All things that are, Are with more spirit chased than enjoy'd. How like a younker or a prodigal The scarfed bark puts from her native bay, Hugg'd and embraced by the strumpet wind! How like the prodigal doth she return, With over-weather'd ribs and ragged sails, Lean, rent and beggar'd by the strumpet wind!	**GRATIANO** That's very true: who leaves the table after a feast With the same hunger he had when he sat down to eat? Does any horse retrace his steps With great care and have the same passion That he felt when he first set out? We are More enthusiastic about the chase than the catch. Just like a young fellow or a reckless spendthrift Is a sailing ship that leaves the harbour, flags flying, Gently and lovingly moved forward by the power of the wind; Then, how she resembles a reckless spendthrift when she returns, With weather- beaten timbers and ragged sails, Worn out, torn and ruined by the wind!
SALARINO Here comes Lorenzo: more of this hereafter.	**SALARINO** Here comes Lorenzo; let's talk about this later.
Enter LORENZO	*Enter LORENZO*
LORENZO Sweet friends, your patience for my long abode; Not I, but my affairs, have made you wait: When you shall please to play the thieves for wives, I'll watch as long for you then. Approach; Here dwells my father Jew. Ho! who's within?	**LORENZO** Dear friends, thank you for your patience whilst waiting for me! I had to attend to business and that's why I'm late. When it's your turn to steal wives for yourselves, I'll wait just as long for you then. Come here; This is where my future father in law, the Jew, lives. Hello! Who's in there?

Enter JESSICA, above, in boy's clothes **JESSICA** Who are you? Tell me, for more certainty, Albeit I'll swear that I do know your tongue. **LORENZO** Lorenzo, and thy love. **JESSICA** Lorenzo, certain, and my love indeed, For who love I so much? And now who knows But you, Lorenzo, whether I am yours? **LORENZO** Heaven and thy thoughts are witness that thou art. **JESSICA** Here, catch this casket; it is worth the pains. I am glad 'tis night, you do not look on me, For I am much ashamed of my exchange: But love is blind and lovers cannot see The pretty follies that themselves commit; For if they could, Cupid himself would blush To see me thus transformed to a boy. **LORENZO** Descend, for you must be my torchbearer. **JESSICA** What, must I hold a candle to my shames? They in themselves, good-sooth, are too too light. Why, 'tis an office of discovery, love; And I should be obscured. **LORENZO** So are you, sweet, Even in the lovely garnish of a boy. But come at once; For the close night doth play the runaway, And we are stay'd for at Bassanio's feast. **JESSICA** I will make fast the doors, and gild myself With some more ducats, and be with you straight. *Exit above*	*Enter JESSICA, above, in boy's clothes* **JESSICA** Who are you? Tell me , so I can be sure, Although, I swear that I recognise your voice. **LORENZO** I am Lorenzo and the one you love. **JESSICA** Lorenzo, definitely and the one I love for sure; Who else do I love so much? And who else, knows Besides you, Lorenzo, whether I am yours? **LORENZO** God in Heaven knows and you know that you are mine. **JESSICA** Here, catch this box; It will be worth the effort. I am glad it's night time, and you can't see me, Because I am very ashamed of my disguise; But love is blind, and lovers don't notice The silly little things that they do, Because, if they did, Cupid himself would blush with embarrassment To see me like this, disguised as a boy. **LORENZO** Come down, because you're going to be my torch-bearer. **JESSICA** What! Do I have to draw attention to my embarrassment? Truthfully, I am only a little embarrassed at being disguised. But it is because my love for you may be revealed That I should be kept hidden. **LORENZO** You are hidden, sweetheart, Very well disguised as a boy. But come along now, For night will soon be upon us, And they're waiting for us at Bassanio's dinner party. **JESSICA** I will lock the doors, and supply myself With some more ducats, and be with you straight away. *EXIT ABOVE*

GRATIANO Now, by my hood, a Gentile and no Jew.	**GRATIANO** Oh my goodness, she can't be a Jew because she's gentle and nice.
LORENZO Beshrew me but I love her heartily; For she is wise, if I can judge of her, And fair she is, if that mine eyes be true, And true she is, as she hath proved herself, And therefore, like herself, wise, fair and true, Shall she be placed in my constant soul.	**LORENZO** Gosh, I love her so much, Because she is wise, if I'm judging her correctly, And she is beautiful, if my eyes can see, And she's genuine and loyal, as she has proven; And so because she is wise, beautiful and loyal, She will be forever in my heart.
Enter JESSICA, below	*Enter JESSICA, below*
What, art thou come? On, gentlemen; away!	Oh, are you ready? Come on gentlemen, let's get going;
Our masquing mates by this time for us stay.	Our masquerading mates are waiting for us.
Exit with Jessica and Salarino	*Exit with Jessica and Salarino*
Enter ANTONIO	*Enter ANTONIO*
ANTONIO Who's there?	**ANTONIO** Who's there?
GRATIANO Signior Antonio!	**GRATIANO** Signoir Antonio?
ANTONIO Fie, fie, Gratiano! where are all the rest?	**ANTONIO** For goodness sake, Gratiano, where's everyone else?
'Tis nine o'clock: our friends all stay for you. No masque to-night: the wind is come about;	It's nine o'clock; our friends are all waiting for you; We're not having the masquerade tonight; the wind is in the right direction;
Bassanio presently will go aboard: I have sent twenty out to seek for you.	Soon Bassanio will set sail; I have sent twenty people to look for you.
GRATIANO I am glad on't: I desire no more delight	**GRATIANO** I am happy about this; nothing could delight me more
Than to be under sail and gone to-night.	Than to be on our way and set sail tonight.
Exeunt	*Exeunt*

Translation of Act 2 Scene 7

ORIGINAL TEXT	MODERN TRANSLATION
Belmont. A room in PORTIA'S house.	**Belmont. A room in PORTIA'S house.**
Flourish of cornets. Enter PORTIA, with the PRINCE OF MOROCCO, and their trains	*Flourish of cornets. Enter PORTIA, with the PRINCE OF MOROCCO, and their trains*
PORTIA Go draw aside the curtains and discover The several caskets to this noble prince. Now make your choice.	**PORTIA** Go and open the curtains and reveal The three boxes to this noble Prince. Now you must choose.
MOROCCO The first, of gold, who this inscription bears, 'Who chooseth me shall gain what many men desire;' The second, silver, which this promise carries, 'Who chooseth me shall get as much as he deserves;' This third, dull lead, with warning all as blunt, 'Who chooseth me must give and hazard all he hath.' How shall I know if I do choose the right?	**MOROCCO** The first one, made of gold, has an inscription which says: 'Whoever chooses me will get what many men desire'. The second one, made of silver, promises this: 'Whoever chooses me will get what he deserves'. This third one, made of dull lead, has a blunt warning which says: 'Whoever chooses me must give and risk all he has'. How can I know how to choose the right one?
PORTIA The one of them contains my picture, prince: If you choose that, then I am yours withal.	**PORTIA** One of them contains my picture, Prince; If you choose that one, then I am yours along with the picture.
MOROCCO Some god direct my judgment! Let me see; I will survey the inscriptions back again. What says this leaden casket? 'Who chooseth me must give and hazard all he hath.' Must give: for what? for lead? hazard for lead? This casket threatens. Men that hazard all Do it in hope of fair advantages: A golden mind stoops not to shows of dross; I'll then nor give nor hazard aught for lead. What says the silver with her virgin hue? 'Who chooseth me shall get as much as he deserves.' As much as he deserves! Pause there, Morocco, And weigh thy value with an even hand: If thou be'st rated by thy estimation, Thou dost deserve enough; and yet enough May not extend so far as to the lady: And yet to be afeard of my deserving	**MOROCCO** Some god please help me to choose the right one ! Let me see; I will study the inscriptions again. What does this lead box say? 'Whoever chooses me must give and risk all he has.' Must give everything - for what? For lead? Risk everything for lead! This box threatens; men who risk everything Do it in the hope of fair gain. A golden mind doesn't stoop so low as to choose something that is worthless; So I won't give or risk anything for lead. What does the silver one , with its virginal colouring, say? 'Whoever chooses me will get what he deserves.' What he deserves! Wait a minute, ,Morocco, And assess your value with a level head. If you're being assessed by your own standards, Then you deserve plenty, and yet plenty May not be enough to deserve the lady; And yet to question whether I deserve her

Were but a weak disabling of myself.	Is to do myself a disservice.
As much as I deserve! Why, that's the lady: I do in birth deserve her, and in fortunes, In graces and in qualities of breeding; But more than these, in love I do deserve. What if I stray'd no further, but chose here? Let's see once more this saying graved in gold	How much do I deserve? Well, that's the lady! By my noble birth I deserve her, and in wealth, In graces and by high breeding; But even more than these, in love I do deserve her. What if I went no further, but chose this one? Let's look once more at this inscription engraved on the gold one:
'Who chooseth me shall gain what many men desire.'	'Whoever chooses me will get what many men desire'.
Why, that's the lady; all the world desires her;	Well, of course, that's the lady! The whole world desires her;
From the four corners of the earth they come, To kiss this shrine, this mortal-breathing saint: The Hyrcanian deserts and the vasty wilds Of wide Arabia are as thoroughfares now For princes to come view fair Portia: The watery kingdom, whose ambitious head Spits in the face of heaven, is no bar To stop the foreign spirits, but they come, As o'er a brook, to see fair Portia.	They come from the four corners of the earth To kiss this shrine, this living, breathing saint. The Hyrcanian deserts and the vast wilderness Of Arabia are roads well travelled now For princes to come to woo beautiful Portia. The wild seas, whose biggest waves Reach up to the heavens, are no deterrent to the foreign suitors, but they come As if traversing a mere stream, in order to see beautiful Portia.
One of these three contains her heavenly picture.	One of these three boxes contains her heavenly picture.
Is't like that lead contains her? 'Twere damnation	Is it likely that the lead box contains her? It would be damnation
To think so base a thought: it were too gross	To contemplate such an unworthy thought; it would be too dreadful
To rib her cerecloth in the obscure grave. Or shall I think in silver she's immured,	To conceal her in an unmarked grave. Or should I decide that she's concealed in the silver box,
Being ten times undervalued to tried gold? O sinful thought! Never so rich a gem Was set in worse than gold. They have in England	Which is ten times less valuable than gold? Oh what a sinful thought! Such a valuable gem Would never be set in anything less valuable than gold. In England
A coin that bears the figure of an angel Stamped in gold, but that's insculp'd upon; But here an angel in a golden bed Lies all within. Deliver me the key: Here do I choose, and thrive I as I may!	There's a coin which carries the figure of an angel Engraved in gold; but that's engraved upon it. But here is an angel in a golden bed Inside this golden box. Give me the key; This is the one I'm choosing and I hope I shall be successful!
PORTIA There, take it, prince; and if my form lie there,	**PORTIA** There, take the key, Prince and if my picture is in there,
Then I am yours.	Then I am yours.
He unlocks the golden casket	*He unlocks the golden casket*
MOROCCO O hell! what have we here? A carrion Death, within whose empty eye There is a written scroll! I'll read the writing.	**MOROCCO** Oh hell! what have we here? A skull and inside the eye socket There is a written scroll! I will read it.
Reads	*Reads*

All that glitters is not gold; Often have you heard that told: Many a man his life hath sold But my outside to behold: Gilded tombs do worms enfold. Had you been as wise as bold, Young in limbs, in judgment old, Your answer had not been inscroll'd: Fare you well; your suit is cold. Cold, indeed; and labour lost: Then, farewell, heat, and welcome, frost! Portia, adieu. I have too grieved a heart To take a tedious leave: thus losers part. *Exit with his train. Flourish of cornets* **PORTIA** A gentle riddance. Draw the curtains, go. Let all of his complexion choose me so. *Exeunt*	'All that glitters is not gold, Often have you heard that told; Many a man has lost his life By looking at the outside. Coffins decorated with gold, contain worms within them. If your wisdom had equalled your boldness, If you'd been young in body, but had the judgement of an old man, You would not have been reading your answer on this scroll. Goodbye, your suit has been unsuccessful.' Cold indeed and unfruitful labour, Then goodbye, sun and welcome , frost. Goodbye Portia! My heart is too grief stricken To prolong my departing; so we go our separate ways. *Exit with his train. Flourish of cornets* **PORTIA** A polite goodbye. Close the curtains, go away. I don't want any man of his skin colour to choose me. *Exeunt*

Translation of Act 2 Scene 8

ORIGINAL TEXT	MODERN TRANSLATION
Venice. A street.	**Venice. A street.**
Enter SALARINO and SALANIO	*Enter SALARINO and SOLANIO*
SALARINO Why, man, I saw Bassanio under sail: With him is Gratiano gone along; And in their ship I am sure Lorenzo is not.	**SALARINO** Well, I saw Bassanio sailing away; And Gratiano has gone with him; And I'm sure that Lorenzo is not with them.
SALANIO The villain Jew with outcries raised the duke, Who went with him to search Bassanio's ship.	**SOLANIO** That villainous Jew made the Duke aware of his complaints, And he went with him to search Bassanio's ship.
SALARINO He came too late, the ship was under sail: But there the duke was given to understand That in a gondola were seen together Lorenzo and his amorous Jessica: Besides, Antonio certified the duke They were not with Bassanio in his ship.	**SALARINO** But he was too late, the ship had already set sail; And then the Duke was informed That, seen together in a gondola Were Lorenzo and his lover Jessica; Anyway, Antonio assured the Duke That they were not with Bassanio on his ship.
SALANIO I never heard a passion so confused, So strange, outrageous, and so variable, As the dog Jew did utter in the streets: 'My daughter! O my ducats! O my daughter! Fled with a Christian! O my Christian ducats! Justice! the law! my ducats, and my daughter! A sealed bag, two sealed bags of ducats, Of double ducats, stolen from me by my daughter! And jewels, two stones, two rich and precious stones, Stolen by my daughter! Justice! find the girl; She hath the stones upon her, and the ducats.'	**SOLANIO** I've never heard such confused rage, As bizzare, outrageous, and as changeable, As that dog, the Jew expressed in the streets. 'My daughter! Oh my ducats! Oh my daughter! Run off with a Christian! Oh my Christian ducats! Justice! The law! My ducats and my daughter! A sealed bag, two sealed bags of ducats, Of double ducats, stolen from me by my daughter! And jewels – two stones, two rich and precious stones, Stolen by my daughter! Justice! Find the girl; She has my stones and ducats on her.'
SALARINO Why, all the boys in Venice follow him, Crying, his stones, his daughter, and his ducats.	**SALARINO** All the boys in Venice were following him, Shouting , his stones, his daughter, and his ducats.
SALANIO Let good Antonio look he keep his day, Or he shall pay for this.	**SOLANIO** I hope Antonio pays his loan back on time, Or he'll pay the price for this.
SALARINO Marry, well remember'd. I reason'd with a Frenchman yesterday, Who told me, in the narrow seas that part The French and English, there miscarried A vessel of our country richly fraught:	**SALARINO** Good point; I chatted with a French man yesterday, Who told me that, in the channel that separates France and England, there sank A Venetian ship which was laden with riches.

I thought upon Antonio when he told me; And wish'd in silence that it were not his.	I thought of Antonio when he told me, And silently hoped that it wasn't his.
SALANIO You were best to tell Antonio what you hear; Yet do not suddenly, for it may grieve him.	**SOLANIO** You'd better tell Antonio about what you heard; But tell him gently, or it could be a shock.
SALARINO A kinder gentleman treads not the earth. I saw Bassanio and Antonio part: Bassanio told him he would make some speed Of his return: he answer'd, 'Do not so; Slubber not business for my sake, Bassanio But stay the very riping of the time; And for the Jew's bond which he hath of me, Let it not enter in your mind of love: Be merry, and employ your chiefest thoughts To courtship and such fair ostents of love As shall conveniently become you there:' And even there, his eye being big with tears, Turning his face, he put his hand behind him, And with affection wondrous sensible He wrung Bassanio's hand; and so they parted.	**SALARINO** You couldn't find a kinder gentleman on this earth. I saw Bassanio and Antonio saying goodbye to each other. Bassanio told him that he'd hurry Back. He responded, ' Don't hurry back; Don't rush your business for my sake, Bassanio, But stay for as long as is needed; And as for the bond which the Jew has committed me to, Don't even let it enter your mind which is focussed on love; Be happy and turn your attention To courtship and affairs of the heart Which will surely come your way'. And then, his eyes filled with tears, And turning his face away, he extended his hand behind him, And with deep, genuine affection He shook Bassanio's hand; and then they went their separate ways.
SALANIO I think he only loves the world for him. I pray thee, let us go and find him out And quicken his embraced heaviness With some delight or other.	**SOLANIO** I think that he's the reason that Antonio loves life. Please, let's go and find him, And relieve his heavy heart With some delight or other.
SALARINO Do we so. *Exeunt*	**SALARINO** Yes, let's do that. *Exeunt*

Translation of Act 2 Scene 9

ORIGINAL TEXT	MODERN TRANSLATION
Belmont. A room in PORTIA'S house.	**Belmont. A room in PORTIA'S house.**
Enter NERISSA with a Servitor	*Enter NERISSA with a Servitor*
NERISSA Quick, quick, I pray thee; draw the curtain straight: The Prince of Arragon hath ta'en his oath, And comes to his election presently.	**NERISSA** Quickly, quickly, please close the curtain immediately; The Prince of Arragon has taken his oath, And he's coming to make his choice shortly.
Flourish of cornets. Enter the PRINCE OF ARRAGON, PORTIA, and their trains	*Flourish of cornets. Enter the PRINCE OF ARRAGON, PORTIA, and their trains*
PORTIA Behold, there stand the caskets, noble prince: If you choose that wherein I am contain'd, Straight shall our nuptial rites be solemnized: But if you fail, without more speech, my lord, You must be gone from hence immediately.	**PORTIA** There are the boxes, noble Prince. If you choose the one that contains my picture, Our marriage ceremony will take place immediately; But if you fail, without another word, my lord, You must leave immediately.
ARRAGON I am enjoin'd by oath to observe three things: First, never to unfold to any one Which casket 'twas I chose; next, if I fail Of the right casket, never in my life To woo a maid in way of marriage: Lastly, If I do fail in fortune of my choice, Immediately to leave you and be gone.	**ARRAGON** I have sworn an oath to three things: First, never to reveal to anyone Which box I chose; next, if I fail To choose the right casket, never in my life To propose marriage to any other woman; Lastly, If I fail to choose the right box, To leave immediately.
PORTIA To these injunctions every one doth swear That comes to hazard for my worthless self.	**PORTIA** Everyone must swear that they commit to these conditions Who comes to gamble on winning me.
ARRAGON And so have I address'd me. Fortune now To my heart's hope! Gold; silver; and base lead. 'Who chooseth me must give and hazard all he hath.' You shall look fairer, ere I give or hazard. What says the golden chest? ha! let me see: 'Who chooseth me shall gain what many men desire.' What many men desire! that 'many' may be meant By the fool multitude, that choose by show,	**ARRAGON** And I have sworn on these rules too. Good luck now Will give me what my heart hopes for! Gold, silver and common lead. Whoever chooses me must give and risk everything he has'. You'll have to look more beautiful before I'll give or risk anything for you. What does the gold box say? Hmm, let's see: ' Whoever chooses me will get what many men desire'. What many men desire – that 'many' may mean That many people are foolish, who choose by outward appearances,

Not learning more than the fond eye doth teach; Which pries not to the interior, but, like the martlet, Builds in the weather on the outward wall, Even in the force and road of casualty.	Not looking beyond what the eye can see; Who don't look at the inside, but, like the swallows, Which build their nests on the outsides of walls, Even though they're more exposed and vulnerable there.
I will not choose what many men desire,	I won't choose what many men desire,
Because I will not jump with common spirits And rank me with the barbarous multitudes. Why, then to thee, thou silver treasure-house; Tell me once more what title thou dost bear: 'Who chooseth me shall get as much as he deserves:' And well said too; for who shall go about To cozen fortune and be honourable Without the stamp of merit? Let none presume	Because I won't jump on the band wagon with those common souls And rank myself with the uncivilised multitudes. So then, it's you, you silver treasure house! Tell me once more what you say. ' Whoever chooses me will get whatever he deserves.' That's a good saying; because who can go around Cheating luck and receive an honour Without genuinely deserving it? No one should expect
To wear an undeserved dignity. O, that estates, degrees and offices Were not derived corruptly, and that clear honour Were purchased by the merit of the wearer! How many then should cover that stand bare!	To receive an undeserved honour. If only property, rank and official positions, Were not obtained corruptly, and that true honour Was only attained by a deserving recipient! How many who're now without honour, would then be honoured!
How many be commanded that command!	How many who're now giving commands would then be receiving them!
How much low peasantry would then be glean'd From the true seed of honour! and how much honour Pick'd from the chaff and ruin of the times To be new-varnish'd! Well, but to my choice:	How many peasants would then be gathered From genuine men of honour! and how many honourable men Picked out from the cast aside chaff, Would be honoured for the first time! Well, I have to make my choice.
'Who chooseth me shall get as much as he deserves.' I will assume desert. Give me a key for this,	'Whoever chooses me shall get whatever he deserves.' I'm assuming that I am deserving. Give me a key for this one,
And instantly unlock my fortunes here.	And in an instant reveal my fate.
He opens the silver casket	*He opens the silver casket*
PORTIA Too long a pause for that which you find there.	**PORTIA** You're taking too long to react to what you found in the box.
ARRAGON What's here? the portrait of a blinking idiot, Presenting me a schedule! I will read it. How much unlike art thou to Portia! How much unlike my hopes and my deservings!	**ARRAGON** What is this? A portrait of a blinking idiot Holding up a scroll! I will read it. You don't look at all like Portia! You don't look at all like what I hoped for and deserve!
'Who chooseth me shall have as much as he deserves.' Did I deserve no more than a fool's head? Is that my prize? are my deserts no better?	'Whoever chooses me shall get what he deserves.' Do I deserve just a fool's head? Is that my prize? Am I worth no more than this?
PORTIA To offend, and judge, are distinct offices And of opposed natures.	**PORTIA** Judging what you deserve and offending you are two very different matters.

ARRAGON What is here? *Reads* The fire seven times tried this: Seven times tried that judgment is, That did never choose amiss. Some there be that shadows kiss; Such have but a shadow's bliss: There be fools alive, I wis, Silver'd o'er; and so was this. Take what wife you will to bed, I will ever be your head: So be gone: you are sped. Still more fool I shall appear By the time I linger here With one fool's head I came to woo, But I go away with two. Sweet, adieu. I'll keep my oath, Patiently to bear my wroth.	**ARRAGON** What does this say? *Reads* 'This box was tested in the fire seven times; Judgement that is tested and refined seven times Will never make a wrong choice. Some people kiss shadows, And they only experience a shadow of joy. There are fools alive with Silver hair, and this is you. Take whatever wife you choose to bed, You will always have a fool's head. So off you go; you are dismissed'. I'll look even more of a fool The longer I stay here. When I came to woo Portia I had the head of a fool, But now I'm leaving with two fools' heads. Sweet lady, goodbye! I'll stand by my oath, And patiently endure my anger.
Exeunt Arragon and train	*Exeunt Arragon and train*
PORTIA Thus hath the candle singed the moth. O, these deliberate fools! when they do choose, They have the wisdom by their wit to lose.	**PORTIA** And so the candle has singed the moth. Oh, these determined fools! When they come to choose, They only have enough wisdom to lose.
NERISSA The ancient saying is no heresy, Hanging and wiving goes by destiny.	**NERISSA** The ancient saying is true: Destiny chooses when you die and when you marry.
PORTIA Come, draw the curtain, Nerissa.	**PORTIA** Come here, close the curtains, Nerrisa.
Enter a Servant	*Enter a servant*
Servant Where is my lady?	**SERVANT** Where is lady Portia?
PORTIA Here: what would my lord?	**PORTIA** Here I am; how can I help you, sir?
Servant Madam, there is alighted at your gate A young Venetian, one that comes before To signify the approaching of his lord; From whom he bringeth sensible regreets, To wit, besides commends and courteous breath, Gifts of rich value. Yet I have not seen So likely an ambassador of love: A day in April never came so sweet, To show how costly summer was at hand, As this fore-spurrer comes before his lord.	**SERVANT** Madam, there is, arrived at your door A young Venetian man, who's come early To announce the approaching of his master, Who sends pleasant greetings; And besides his courteous words and demeanour, He also sends valuable gifts. I've not yet seen Such a promising ambassador of love. As an April day comes so sweetly To show how rich a summer is about to arrive Is how this fore- runner to his master arrives.

PORTIA No more, I pray thee: I am half afeard Thou wilt say anon he is some kin to thee, Thou spend'st such high-day wit in praising him. Come, come, Nerissa; for I long to see Quick Cupid's post that comes so mannerly. **NERISSA** Bassanio, lord Love, if thy will it be! *Exeunt*	**PORTIA** Don't say anything else, please; I am half afraid That in a minute you'll say that he's some relative of yours, You praise him so very highly. Come on, come on, Nerissa, I can't wait to see Cupid's delivery that's arrived so courteously. **NERISSA** I really hope that it's Bassanio, the Lord of Love! *exeunt*

Translation of Act 3 Scene 1

ORIGINAL TEXT	MODERN TRANSLATION
Venice. A street.	**Venice. A street.**
Enter SALANIO and SALARINO	*Enter SALANIO and SALARINO*
SALANIO Now, what news on the Rialto?	**SOLANIO** So then, what's the news on the Rialto?
SALARINO Why, yet it lives there uncheck'd that Antonio hath a ship of rich lading wrecked on the narrow seas; the Goodwins, I think they call the place; a very dangerous flat and fatal, where the carcasses of many a tall ship lie buried, as they say, if my gossip Report be an honest woman of her word.	**SALARINO** Well, rumour is rife that Antonio has a ship, full of valuable cargo, shipwrecked on the narrow seas; I think it's called the Goodwin sands, a very dangerous sandbar, where it's said, the wrecks of many sailing ships lay buried, if the rumour turns out to be true.
SALANIO I would she were as lying a gossip in that as ever knapped ginger or made her neighbours believe she wept for the death of a third husband. But it is true, without any slips of prolixity or crossing the plain highway of talk, that the good Antonio, the honest Antonio,--O that I had a title good enough to keep his name company!--	**SOLANIO** I really hope that this rumour is a lie, like a rumour spread by a widow, convincing her neighbours that she cried over the death of her third husband. But it is true, without any exaggerating, when I say the good Antonio, the honest Antonio. Oh if I could have a reputation as good as Antonio has!-
SALARINO Come, the full stop.	**SALARINO** Come on, what are you saying?
SALANIO Ha! what sayest thou? Why, the end is, he hath lost a ship.	**SOLANIO** What are you saying? Well, the point is, he has lost a ship.
SALARINO I would it might prove the end of his losses.	**SALARINO** I really hope that's all he loses.
SALANIO Let me say 'amen' betimes, lest the devil cross my prayer, for here he comes in the likeness of a Jew.	**SOLANIO** Let me say 'amen' early, incase the devil blocks my prayer, because here comes the devil disguised as a Jew.
Enter SHYLOCK	*Enter SHYLOCK*
How now, Shylock! what news among the merchants?	How's it going, Shylock? What's the news from the merchants?
SHYLOCK You know, none so well, none so well as you, of my daughter's flight.	**SHYLOCK** You knew, no one knew as well, no one as well as you did, about my daughter running away.

SALARINO That's certain: I, for my part, knew the tailor that made the wings she flew withal.	**SALARINO** That's true; I admit that I knew the tailor who made the disguise she wore when she ran away.
SALANIO And Shylock, for his own part, knew the bird was fledged; and then it is the complexion of them all to leave the dam.	**SOLANIO** And Shylock must admit that he knew that his daughter was ready to fledge the nest; and that it is natural for all children to leave their parents.
SHYLOCK She is damned for it.	**SHYLOCK** She'll go to hell for this.
SALANIO That's certain, if the devil may be her judge.	**SALARINO** That's for certain , if the devil is judging her.
SHYLOCK My own flesh and blood to rebel!	**SHYLOCK** My own flesh and blood has rebelled!
SALANIO Out upon it, old carrion! rebels it at these years?	**SOLANIO** What, old man! Rebelling at this age?
SHYLOCK I say, my daughter is my flesh and blood.	**SHYLOCK** I mean that my daughter is my flesh and blood.
SALARINO There is more difference between thy flesh and hers than between jet and ivory; more between your bloods than there is between red wine and rhenish. But tell us, do you hear whether Antonio have had any loss at sea or no?	**SALARINO** There is more difference between your flesh and hers than between coal and ivory; your blood and her blood are more different then red and white wines. But tell us have you heard whether Antonio has had any losses at sea or not?
SHYLOCK There I have another bad match: a bankrupt, a prodigal, who dare scarce show his head on the Rialto; a beggar, that was used to come so smug upon the mart; let him look to his bond: he was wont to call me usurer; let him look to his bond: he was wont to lend money for a Christian courtesy; let him look to his bond.	**SHYLOCK** There's another mismatch: a bankrupt, a spendthrift, who can hardly dare to show his face on the Rialto; a beggar who used to be so smug when in the business market. Let him think about our contract. He liked to call me a loan shark; let him look at his legal contract. He liked to lend money as a Christian kindness; let him think about his legal commitment.
SALARINO Why, I am sure, if he forfeit, thou wilt not take his flesh: what's that good for?	**SALARINO** But surely, if he can't pay, you won't take his flesh? What good is that to anyone?
SHYLOCK To bait fish withal: if it will feed nothing else, it will feed my revenge. He hath disgraced me, and hindered me half a million; laughed at my losses, mocked at my gains, scorned my nation, thwarted my bargains, cooled my friends, heated mine enemies; and what's his reason? I am a Jew. Hath not a Jew eyes? hath not a Jew hands, organs, dimensions, senses, affections, passions? fed with the same food, hurt with the same weapons, subject	**SHYLOCK** I will use it for fish bait. If it feeds nothing else, it will feed my revenge. He has insulted me and lost me half a million ducats; laughed at my losses, mocked my earnings, humiliated my race, sabotaged my deals, turned my friends against me, inflamed my enemies. And what's his reason? I am a Jew. Doesn't a Jew have eyes? Doesn't a Jew have hands, organs, human dimensions, senses, feelings, passions, get fed with the same food, hurt by the same weapons, fall ill with the same diseases, get healed by the

to the same diseases, healed by the same means, warmed and cooled by the same winter and summer, as a Christian is? If you prick us, do we not bleed? if you tickle us, do we not laugh? if you poison us, do we not die? and if you wrong us, shall we not revenge? If we are like you in the rest, we will resemble you in that. If a Jew wrong a Christian, what is his humility? Revenge. If a Christian wrong a Jew, what should his sufferance be by Christian example? Why, revenge. The villany you teach me, I will execute, and it shall go hard but I will better the instruction.	same medicines, get warmed and cooled by the same winter and summer, as a Christian? If you prick us, don't we bleed? If you tickle us, don't we laugh? If you poison us, don't we die? And if you treat us badly, won't we take revenge? If we're like you in every other way, we'll be like you in that way too. If a Jew wrongs a Christian, what is his humble response? Revenge. If a Christian wrongs a Jew, what should his response be if he follows Christian example? Revenge of course. The bad ways you've taught me I will put into practice; it will be harsh but I will outdo my instructors.
Enter a Servant	*Enter a Servant*
Servant Gentlemen, my master Antonio is at his house and desires to speak with you both.	**Servant** Gentlemen, my master Antonio is at his house and would like to speak with both of you.
SALARINO We have been up and down to seek him.	**SALARINO** We've been looking everywhere for him.
Enter TUBAL	*Enter TUBAL*
SALANIO Here comes another of the tribe: a third cannot be matched, unless the devil himself turn Jew.	**SOLANIO** Here comes another one from that tribe of Jews; you couldn't find a third one unless the devil himself became a Jew.
Exeunt SALANIO, SALARINO, and Servant	*Exeunt SALANIO, SALARINO, and Servant*
SHYLOCK How now, Tubal! what news from Genoa? hast thou found my daughter?	**SHYLOCK** How's it going, Tubal? What's the news from Genoa? Have you found my daughter?
TUBAL I often came where I did hear of her, but cannot find her.	**TUBAL** I went to many places where I heard news of her whereabouts, but I can't find her.
SHYLOCK Why, there, there, there, there! a diamond gone, cost me two thousand ducats in Frankfort! The curse never fell upon our nation till now; I never felt it till now: two thousand ducats in that; and other precious, precious jewels. I would my daughter were dead at my foot, and the jewels in her ear! would she were hearsed at my foot, and the ducats in her coffin! No news of them? Why, so: and I know not what's spent in the search: why, thou loss upon loss! the thief gone with so much, and so much to find the thief; and no satisfaction, no revenge: nor no in luck stirring but what lights on my shoulders; no sighs but of my breathing; no tears but of my shedding.	**SHYLOCK** Oh, Oh Oh! A diamond has gone, which cost me two thousand ducats in Frankfort! It's as if only now the curse has fallen upon the Jews; I never experienced it until now. Two thousand ducats in that diamond alone and other precious, precious jewels. I wish that my daughter was dead at my feet, with the jewels in her ears; wish that she was in her coffin at my feet and the ducats in her coffin! No news of them? How's that then – and I don't know how much I'm spending searching for her. Loss upon loss! The thief went with so much, and I'm spending so much to find the thief; and no success, no revenge; and no bad luck for anyone except for me; no sighing but my own; the only tears shed are my own tears!

TUBAL Yes, other men have ill luck too: Antonio, as I heard in Genoa,--	**TUBAL** Yes, other men do have bad luck too: Antonio, according to what I heard in Genoa –
SHYLOCK What, what, what? ill luck, ill luck?	**SHYLOCK** What, what, what? Bad luck, bad luck?
TUBAL Hath an argosy cast away, coming from Tripolis.	**TUBAL** A ship coming from Tripolis has been shipwrecked.
SHYLOCK I thank God, I thank God. Is't true, is't true?	**SHYLOCK** I thank God, I thank God. Is it true, is it true?
TUBAL I spoke with some of the sailors that escaped the wreck.	**TUBAL** I spoke with some of the sailors who escaped from the shipwreck.
SHYLOCK I thank thee, good Tubal: good news, good news! ha, ha! where? in Genoa?	**SHYLOCK** Thank you, good Tubal. Good news, good news – ha ha! – Where in Genoa?
TUBAL Your daughter spent in Genoa, as I heard, in one night fourscore ducats.	**TUBAL** I heard that your daughter spent eighty ducats in one night in Genoa.
SHYLOCK Thou stickest a dagger in me: I shall never see my gold again: fourscore ducats at a sitting! fourscore ducats!	**SHYLOCK** You're sticking the knife in – I'll never see my gold again. Eighty ducats in one night! Eighty ducats!
TUBAL There came divers of Antonio's creditors in my company to Venice, that swear he cannot choose but break.	**TUBAL** Various of Antonio's creditors travelled with me to Venice and they swear that he'll have no choice but to go bankrupt.
SHYLOCK I am very glad of it: I'll plague him; I'll torture him: I am glad of it.	**SHYLOCK** I am very glad about that; I'll plague him, I'll torture him; I am very glad about that.
TUBAL One of them showed me a ring that he had of your daughter for a monkey.	**TUBAL** One of them showed me a ring that your daughter gave him in exchange for a monkey.
SHYLOCK Out upon her! Thou torturest me, Tubal: it was my turquoise; I had it of Leah when I was a bachelor: I would not have given it for a wilderness of monkeys.	**SHYLOCK** Damn her! You're torturing me, Tubal. It was my turquoise one; Leah gave it to me when I was single; I would not have given it away for a jungle of monkeys.
TUBAL But Antonio is certainly undone.	**TUBAL** But Antonio is definitely ruined.
SHYLOCK Nay, that's true, that's very true. Go, Tubal, fee me an officer; bespeak him a fortnight before. I will have the heart of him, if he forfeit; for, were he out of Venice, I can make what merchandise I	**SHYLOCK** That's true; that's very true. Go, Tubal and get a police officer; prepare him two weeks in advance. I will have Antonio's heart, if he doesn't pay his debt; because if he was out of Venice, I could do business

will. Go, go, Tubal, and meet me at our synagogue; go, good Tubal; at our synagogue, Tubal. *Exeunt*	however I want to. Go, Tubal and meet me at our synagogue; go, good Tubal; see you at the synagogue, Tubal. *Exeunt*

Translation of Act 3 Scene 2

ORIGINAL TEXT	MODERN TRANSLATION
Belmont. A room in PORTIA'S house.	**Belmont. A room in PORTIA'S house.**
Enter BASSANIO, PORTIA, GRATIANO, NERISSA, and Attendants	*Enter BASSANIO, PORTIA, GRATIANO, NERISSA, and Attendants*
PORTIA I pray you, tarry: pause a day or two Before you hazard; for, in choosing wrong, I lose your company: therefore forbear awhile. There's something tells me, but it is not love, I would not lose you; and you know yourself, Hate counsels not in such a quality. But lest you should not understand me well,-- And yet a maiden hath no tongue but thought,-- I would detain you here some month or two Before you venture for me. I could teach you How to choose right, but I am then forsworn; So will I never be: so may you miss me; But if you do, you'll make me wish a sin, That I had been forsworn. Beshrew your eyes, They have o'erlook'd me and divided me; One half of me is yours, the other half yours, Mine own, I would say; but if mine, then yours, And so all yours. O, these naughty times Put bars between the owners and their rights! And so, though yours, not yours. Prove it so, Let fortune go to hell for it, not I. I speak too long; but 'tis to peize the time, To eke it and to draw it out in length, To stay you from election.	**PORTIA** Please stay a while; wait for a day or two Before you make your choice; because if you choose the wrong box, I'll lose your company; so delay for a while. Something tells me - but it is not love – That I don't want to lose you; and you know yourself Hatred wouldn't cause me to feel this way. But incase you don't understand me clearly – Even though a young woman should not voice her feelings – I would like to keep you here for a month or two Before you try to win me. I could teach you How to choose correctly, but I have sworn an oath; So I will never be able to help you choose; so you may lose me; But if you do choose wrongly, you'll make me wish that it was to a sin, To which I'd sworn an oath. Curse your eyes! They have looked at me and divided me in two; One half of me is yours, and the other half is yours – My own half it is; but if it is mine, then it is yours, And so all of me is yours. Oh! These difficult times Put obstacles between the owners and what is rightfully theirs; And so, although I am yours, I am not yet yours. If that happens, Let fortune go to hell, not me. I am talking too much, but I'm playing for time, Making it last, drawing it out, To delay you from making your choice.
BASSANIO Let me choose For as I am, I live upon the rack.	**BASSANIO** Let me choose; Because as it is, I feel as if I'm being tortured.
PORTIA Upon the rack, Bassanio! then confess What treason there is mingled with your love.	**PORTIA** Tortured, Bassanio? Then confess What treason is there mingling with your love.
BASSANIO None but that ugly treason of mistrust, Which makes me fear the enjoying of my love:	**BASSANIO** There's none at all, except the ugly treason of doubt, Which makes me worry that I'll never enjoy your love; There would be peace and harmony

There may as well be amity and life 'Tween snow and fire, as treason and my love.	Between snow and fire, if there was any treason in my love.
PORTIA Ay, but I fear you speak upon the rack, Where men enforced do speak anything.	**PORTIA** But I'm afraid you're speaking under torture, When men will say anything under duress.
BASSANIO Promise me life, and I'll confess the truth.	**BASSANIO** Promise that you'll let me live and I'll confess the truth.
PORTIA Well then, confess and live.	**PORTIA** OK then, confess and I'll let you live.
BASSANIO 'Confess' and 'love' Had been the very sum of my confession: O happy torment, when my torturer Doth teach me answers for deliverance! But let me to my fortune and the caskets.	**BASSANIO** 'Confess' and 'love' That's the sum total of my confession. Oh happy torment, when my torturer Tells me what to say to be freed! But let try my luck with the boxes.
PORTIA Away, then! I am lock'd in one of them: If you do love me, you will find me out. Nerissa and the rest, stand all aloof. Let music sound while he doth make his choice; Then, if he lose, he makes a swan-like end, Fading in music: that the comparison	**PORTIA** Off you go then; I am locked in one of them. If you love me, you will find me. Nerissa and all the rest of you, give him some space; Play some music while he's making his choice; Then, if he loses, it will be his swan-song, As he fades away at the end of the music. So that the comparison
May stand more proper, my eye shall be the stream	Is even more life- like, my crying eyes will provide the river
And watery death-bed for him. He may win; And what is music then? Then music is	For his watery exit. But he may win; And what sort of music should be played then? The music should
Even as the flourish when true subjects bow	Be like the heralding music which sounds forth when loyal subjects bow
To a new-crowned monarch: such it is As are those dulcet sounds in break of day That creep into the dreaming bridegroom's ear, And summon him to marriage. Now he goes,	To a newly crowned king; it should be like The sweet sounds of daybreak That gently wake a dreaming bridegroom And call him to the church on his wedding day. Bassanio's going to the boxes now,
With no less presence, but with much more love, Than young Alcides, when he did redeem The virgin tribute paid by howling Troy	With no less dignity, but with much more love, Than young Hercules, when he saved The princess Hesione who was given as payment for Troy's walls
To the sea-monster: I stand for sacrifice The rest aloof are the Dardanian wives, With bleared visages, come forth to view The issue of the exploit. Go, Hercules! Live thou, I live: with much, much more dismay I view the fight than thou that makest the fray.	To the sea monster. I'll play her part; The other bystanders are Trojan wives, With blurred faces, who've come out to watch The outcome of the deed. Go, Hercules! If you live, then I will live. It is much more distressing For me to watch the battle, than it is for you participating in it.
Music, whilst BASSANIO comments on the caskets to himself	*Music, whilst BASSANIO comments on the caskets to himself*

SONG.	SONG.
Tell me where is fancy bred,	Tell me where does desire start,
Or in the heart, or in the head?	In the heart or in the head,
How begot, how nourished?	How is it created and how is it nurtured?
Reply, reply.	Answer me, answer me.
It is engender'd in the eyes,	It starts in the eyes,
With gazing fed; and fancy dies	Sustained by gazing; and desire dies
In the cradle where it lies.	All too soon, before it's able to grow.
Let us all ring fancy's knell	Let us ring the death knell of our desire:
I'll begin it,--Ding, dong, bell.	I'll begin – Ding, dong, bell.
ALL	**ALL**
Ding, dong, bell.	Ding, dong, bell.
BASSANIO	**BASSANIO**
So may the outward shows be least themselves:	What appears to be great on the outside may actually be worth very little;
The world is still deceived with ornament.	People are still deceived by outward appearances.
In law, what plea so tainted and corrupt,	In a court of law, doesn't a dishonest, false plea
But, being seasoned with a gracious voice,	Presented with a voice that sounds honest and good,
Obscures the show of evil? In religion,	Hide the evil reality? In religion,
What damned error, but some sober brow	An evil sin will, by someone who appears to have integrity,
Will bless it and approve it with a text,	Be justified by scripture,
Hiding the grossness with fair ornament?	Covering up evil with the appearance of good?
There is no vice so simple but assumes	There is no sin however small that isn't able
Some mark of virtue on his outward parts:	To somehow give some appearance of good.
How many cowards, whose hearts are all as false	How may cowards, whose hearts are not genuinely strong
As stairs of sand, wear yet upon their chins	Sport beards upon their chins
The beards of Hercules and frowning Mars;	Beards like Hercules and Mars, the god of war;
Who, inward search'd, have livers white as milk;	Who are actually lilly- livered in reality!
And these assume but valour's excrement	And these put on only the waste products of bravery
To render them redoubted! Look on beauty,	To make themselves appear formidable. Likewise, beauty
And you shall see 'tis purchased by the weight;	It is purchased by the ounce, as cosmetics,
Which therein works a miracle in nature,	Which, when it's applied, works miracles,
Making them lightest that wear most of it:	Bringing the least respect to those who wear it the most;
So are those crisped snaky golden locks	Just the same as long flowing golden hair
Which make such wanton gambols with the wind,	Which moves so seductively in the breeze
Upon supposed fairness, often known	Upon a beautiful head often known
To be the dowry of a second head,	To be the second head that's worn this hair (a wig) –
The skull that bred them in the sepulchre.	The original head which grew the hair, now a skull in the grave.
Thus ornament is but the guiled shore	So, outward appearance is like the beautiful shoreline
To a most dangerous sea; the beauteous scarf	Of a most dangerous sea; the beautiful scarf
Veiling an Indian beauty; in a word,	Concealing an Indian beauty; in short
The seeming truth which cunning times put on	Things that appear true are cunningly presented
To entrap the wisest. Therefore, thou gaudy gold,	To trap the wisest of people. So, you gaudy gold box,
Hard food for Midas, I will none of thee;	Like gold which Midas couldn't eat, I will not choose you;

Nor none of thee, thou pale and common drudge 'Tween man and man: but thou, thou meagre lead, Which rather threatenest than dost promise aught, Thy paleness moves me more than eloquence; And here choose I; joy be the consequence! **PORTIA** [Aside] How all the other passions fleet to air, As doubtful thoughts, and rash-embraced despair, And shuddering fear, and green-eyed jealousy! O love, Be moderate; allay thy ecstasy, In measure rein thy joy; scant this excess. I feel too much thy blessing: make it less, For fear I surfeit. **BASSANIO** What find I here? *Opening the leaden casket* Fair Portia's counterfeit! What demi-god Hath come so near creation? Move these eyes? Or whether, riding on the balls of mine, Seem they in motion? Here are sever'd lips, Parted with sugar breath: so sweet a bar Should sunder such sweet friends. Here in her hairs The painter plays the spider and hath woven A golden mesh to entrap the hearts of men, Faster than gnats in cobwebs; but her eyes,-- How could he see to do them? having made one, Methinks it should have power to steal both his And leave itself unfurnish'd. Yet look, how far The substance of my praise doth wrong this shadow In underprizing it, so far this shadow Doth limp behind the substance. Here's the scroll, The continent and summary of my fortune. *Reads* You that choose not by the view, Chance as fair and choose as true! Since this fortune falls to you, Be content and seek no new, If you be well pleased with this And hold your fortune for your bliss, Turn you where your lady is And claim her with a loving kiss.	Nor will I choose you, silver, the same pale and common colour as coins Used by men as common currency; but you, humble lead box, Which appears more threatening than promising, Your ordinariness moves me more than words can express, And this is my choice. May the result be joy! **PORTIA** (aside) All my other emotions are flying away, Like feelings of doubt and foolish despair, Trembling fear and green eyed jealousy! Oh love, I must calm down, not be so ecstatic, Control the flow of joy, not be too excessive! I'm experiencing love's blessing too much. Calm it down, Because I'm scared of loving too much. **BASSANIO** What do I find here? *Opening the leaden casket* A picture of beautiful Portia! What demi-god Has captured her likeness so well? Are her eyes moving? Or is it that when my eyes move Hers seem to move too? Here are her separated lips, Parted with sweet breath; such a sweet barrier Keeping such sweet friends apart. Here in her hair The artist is like a spider and has woven a web Of golden mesh to trap the hearts of men Faster than gnats in a cobweb. But her eyes – How could he concentrate enough to paint them? Having painted one of her eyes, I think that it would have the power to captivate both of his eyes, And leave the other eye unpainted. Yet look how The expression of my praise is inadequate for this picture Just as the picture is insufficient praise for the real woman herself. Here's the scroll, That tells me what my fate is. *Reads* You who don't choose by appearances, Have good luck and choose the right one! Since this destiny falls to you, Be content and don't look for any other. If you're delighted with this, And consider your destiny to be perfect happiness, Then turn to your lady And claim her with a loving kiss.'

A gentle scroll. Fair lady, by your leave; I come by note, to give and to receive. Like one of two contending in a prize, That thinks he hath done well in people's eyes, Hearing applause and universal shout, Giddy in spirit, still gazing in a doubt Whether these pearls of praise be his or no; So, thrice fair lady, stand I, even so; As doubtful whether what I see be true, Until confirm'd, sign'd, ratified by you. **PORTIA** You see me, Lord Bassanio, where I stand, Such as I am: though for myself alone I would not be ambitious in my wish, To wish myself much better; yet, for you I would be trebled twenty times myself; A thousand times more fair, ten thousand times more rich; That only to stand high in your account, I might in virtue, beauties, livings, friends, Exceed account; but the full sum of me Is sum of something, which, to term in gross, Is an unlesson'd girl, unschool'd, unpractised; Happy in this, she is not yet so old But she may learn; happier than this, She is not bred so dull but she can learn; Happiest of all is that her gentle spirit Commits itself to yours to be directed, As from her lord, her governor, her king. Myself and what is mine to you and yours Is now converted: but now I was the lord Of this fair mansion, master of my servants, Queen o'er myself: and even now, but now, This house, these servants and this same myself Are yours, my lord: I give them with this ring; Which when you part from, lose, or give away, Let it presage the ruin of your love And be my vantage to exclaim on you. **BASSANIO** Madam, you have bereft me of all words, Only my blood speaks to you in my veins; And there is such confusion in my powers, As after some oration fairly spoke By a beloved prince, there doth appear Among the buzzing pleased multitude; Where every something, being blent together, Turns to a wild of nothing, save of joy,	A kind message. Beautiful lady, with your permission; I come, authorised by this note, to give and receive a kiss. Like someone fighting to win a prize, Who thinks that he's done well in people's eyes, Hearing clapping and everyone shouting, In high spirits, but still unsure Whether all the applause and praise is for him or not; So, very beautiful lady, I am standing here, Wondering whether it can be true, Until signed, sealed and delivered by you. **PORTIA** You see me, Lord Bassanio, standing here, Just as I am. Though for my own sake I would not have any ambitions To be much better, but for your sake I wish I were sixty times more than myself, A thousand times more beautiful and ten thousand times richer, Just so that I would be highly regarded by you So that my good characteristics, beauty, possessions and friends, Would be too many to count. But the whole of me Is something, which in total amounts to, An innocent girl, uneducated and inexperienced; Content to be like this, as she is not too old To learn; even happier That she's not stupid and can learn; But happiest of all that her gentle spirit Gives itself to you to be guided, By her lord, her master, her king. Myself and everything I have to you I now give. Until now I was the lord Of this lovely mansion, master of my servants, Queen over myself; and from this time, right this moment, This house, these servants and my very self, Are yours – my lord's. I give them to you with this ring, Which if you ever give away or lose, Will be a sign of the ruin of your love, And it will be my place to be angry with you. **BASSANIO** Madam, you have left me completely lost for words; Only the lifeblood within me communicates with you; And my emotions are in turmoil Just like after a beautiful speech is given By a beloved prince and it causes A thrilled, excited crowd, Where every sound, blended together, Produces a wild celebration of nothing but joy

Express'd and not express'd. But when this ring Parts from this finger, then parts life from hence: O, then be bold to say Bassanio's dead!	Both expressible and inexpressible. But if this ring ever Departs from this finger, then life will depart from me; If that ever happens, you can be sure it's because I'm dead!
NERISSA My lord and lady, it is now our time, That have stood by and seen our wishes prosper, To cry, good joy: good joy, my lord and lady!	**NERISSA** My lord and lady, now is the time For those who have stood watching and seen our dreams come true To shout 'Congratulations'. 'Great joy, my lord and lady'
GRATIANO My lord Bassanio and my gentle lady, I wish you all the joy that you can wish; For I am sure you can wish none from me: And when your honours mean to solemnize The bargain of your faith, I do beseech you, Even at that time I may be married too.	**GRATIANO** My lord Bassanio and my dear lady, I wish you all the joy you could wish for, Because I'm sure you don't need any joy from me; And when the time comes for you to make your wedding vows Before God, I earnestly ask you If at that time I could be married too.
BASSANIO With all my heart, so thou canst get a wife.	**BASSANIO** Yes, absolutely, if you can find a wife.
GRATIANO I thank your lordship, you have got me one. My eyes, my lord, can look as swift as yours: You saw the mistress, I beheld the maid; You loved, I loved for intermission. No more pertains to me, my lord, than you. Your fortune stood upon the casket there, And so did mine too, as the matter falls; For wooing here until I sweat again, And sweating until my very roof was dry With oaths of love, at last, if promise last, I got a promise of this fair one here To have her love, provided that your fortune Achieved her mistress.	**GRATIANO** Thanks to you, my lord, I have found one My eyes, my lord, can look as quickly as yours: You saw the mistress, and I discovered the maid; You fell in love, and I fell in love; because delaying Is not my style, my lord, any more than it is yours. Your fate depended on those boxes there, And so did mine, as it turned out; After chasing her persistently, And declaring, until my mouth was dry, My undying love, at last – if she keeps her promise – This beautiful woman here promised Me her love, provided that your fate Won her mistress as your wife.
PORTIA Is this true, Nerissa?	**PORTIA** Is this true, Nerissa?
NERISSA Madam, it is, so you stand pleased withal.	**NERISSA** Madam, it is, if that's alright with you.
BASSANIO And do you, Gratiano, mean good faith?	**BASSANIO** And Gratiano, are you serious about this?
GRATIANO Yes, faith, my lord.	**GRATIANO** Yes, very serious, my lord.
BASSANIO Our feast shall be much honour'd in your marriage.	**BASSANIO** We will be greatly honoured if you share our wedding ceremony.

GRATIANO
We'll play with them the first boy for a thousand ducats.

NERISSA
What, and stake down?

GRATIANO
No; we shall ne'er win at that sport, and stake down. But who comes here? Lorenzo and his infidel? What, and my old Venetian friend SALARINO?

Enter LORENZO, JESSICA, and SALARINO, a Messenger from Venice

BASSANIO
Lorenzo and SALARINO, welcome hither;
If that the youth of my new interest here
Have power to bid you welcome. By your leave,
I bid my very friends and countrymen,
Sweet Portia, welcome.

PORTIA
So do I, my lord:
They are entirely welcome.

LORENZO
I thank your honour. For my part, my lord,
My purpose was not to have seen you here;
But meeting with SALARINO by the way,
He did entreat me, past all saying nay,
To come with him along.

SALARINO
I did, my lord;
And I have reason for it. Signior Antonio
Commends him to you.

Gives Bassanio a letter

BASSANIO
Ere I ope his letter,
I pray you, tell me how my good friend doth.

SALARINO
Not sick, my lord, unless it be in mind;
Nor well, unless in mind: his letter there
Will show you his estate.

GRATIANO
Nerissa, cheer yon stranger; bid her welcome.
Your hand, SALARINO: what's the news from Venice?
How doth that royal merchant, good Antonio?

GRATIANO
We'll have a bet with them: a thousand ducats that we'll have a son first.

NERISSA
What, do you want to lay a stake now?

GRATIANO
No; we'll never win the bet if I lay down my stake – But who's this coming? Lorenzo and his infidel girlfriend? What, and my old Venetian friend, SALARINO!

Enter LORENZO, JESSICA, and SALARINO, a Messenger from Venice

BASSANIO
Lorenzo and SALARINO, welcome here,
If my recent belonging to this establishment
Permits me to welcome you. With your permission,
I welcome my very good friends and countrymen,
Sweet Portia.

PORTIA
I do too, my lord;
They're extremely welcome.

LORENZO
Thank you sir. For my part, my lord,
I wasn't intending to come to see you;
But when I bumped into SALARINO by chance,
He persuaded me, despite my reluctance,
To come along here with him.

SALARINO
I did, my lord,
And with good reason. Signior Antonio
Commends him to you.

Gives Bassanio a letter

BASSANIO
Before I open this letter,
Please tell me how my good friend is.

SALARINO
He's not ill, my lord, except for in his troubled mind;
He's not well, because of his troubles; his letter
Will explain to you his situation.

GRATIANO
Nerissa, welcome this stranger;
Welcome, SALARINO. What's the news from Venice?
How's that great merchant, good Antonio?
I know that he'll be pleased we've been successful:

I know he will be glad of our success; We are the Jasons, we have won the fleece.	We are like Jasons (of the Argonauts) and we've won the golden fleece.
SALARINO I would you had won the fleece that he hath lost.	**SALARINO** I wish you'd won the fleece that he's lost.
PORTIA There are some shrewd contents in yon same paper, That steals the colour from Bassanio's cheek: Some dear friend dead; else nothing in the world Could turn so much the constitution Of any constant man. What, worse and worse! With leave, Bassanio: I am half yourself, And I must freely have the half of anything That this same paper brings you.	**PORTIA** There is some bad news contained in that letter Which has made Bassanio go as white as a sheet: A close friend must have died, because nothing in the world Could have such a drastic effect On any man. What, is there even worse news! Please Bassanio: I am your other half, And so I must, without question, bear half of any bad news That this letter brings you
BASSANIO O sweet Portia, Here are a few of the unpleasant'st words That ever blotted paper! Gentle lady, When I did first impart my love to you, I freely told you, all the wealth I had Ran in my veins, I was a gentleman; And then I told you true: and yet, dear lady, Rating myself at nothing, you shall see How much I was a braggart. When I told you My state was nothing, I should then have told you That I was worse than nothing; for, indeed, I have engaged myself to a dear friend, Engaged my friend to his mere enemy, To feed my means. Here is a letter, lady; The paper as the body of my friend, And every word in it a gaping wound, Issuing life-blood. But is it true, SALARINO? Have all his ventures fail'd? What, not one hit? From Tripolis, from Mexico and England, From Lisbon, Barbary and India? And not one vessel 'scape the dreadful touch Of merchant-marring rocks?	**BASSANIO** Oh, sweet Portia, Here are a few of the most unpleasant words That ever blighted a piece of paper! Gentle lady, When I first gave my love to you, I freely told you that all the wealth I possessed Ran within my veins – I was a gentleman; And what I told you was true. And yet, dear lady, By rating myself as nothing, you will soon see How much I was bragging. When I told you That I had no money, I should have told you That I had less than nothing; because I have borrowed money from a dear friend, Who, in turn, has borrowed money from his actual enemy, In order to help me. Here is the letter, lady, The paper is like my friend's body, And every word in it is like a gaping wound Bleeding profusely. But is it true, SALARINO? Have all of his business ventures failed? Not one of them successful? From Tripolis, from Mexico, and England, From Lisbon, Barbary and India, And hasn't even one ship escaped the dreadful Lethal rocks?
SALARINO Not one, my lord. Besides, it should appear, that if he had The present money to discharge the Jew, He would not take it. Never did I know A creature, that did bear the shape of man, So keen and greedy to confound a man: He plies the duke at morning and at night, And doth impeach the freedom of the state,	**SALARINO** No, not even one, my lord. Anyway, it looks as if, even if he had The money now to pay the Jew, He would not take it. I have never known A creature in the form of a human being So eager and desperate to destroy a man. He pursues the Duke morning and night, Calling into question the integrity of the freedom of the state, If they deny him justice. Twenty merchants,

If they deny him justice: twenty merchants, The duke himself, and the magnificoes Of greatest port, have all persuaded with him; But none can drive him from the envious plea Of forfeiture, of justice and his bond.	The Duke himself, and the eminent nobles Of great Venice, have all tried to reason with him; But no-one can divert him from the spiteful demand To have the forfeit paid, for justice and his contract.
JESSICA When I was with him I have heard him swear To Tubal and to Chus, his countrymen, That he would rather have Antonio's flesh Than twenty times the value of the sum That he did owe him: and I know, my lord, If law, authority and power deny not, It will go hard with poor Antonio.	**JESSICA** When I was with him, I heard him swear To Tubal and to Chus, his fellow Jews, That he'd rather have Antonio's flesh Than twenty times the amount of money That Antonio owes him; and I know, my lord, That if the law with its authority and power does not intervene, Then it will be a bad outcome for poor Antonio.
PORTIA Is it your dear friend that is thus in trouble?	**PORTIA** Is it your dear friend who is in this trouble?
BASSANIO The dearest friend to me, the kindest man, The best-condition'd and unwearied spirit In doing courtesies, and one in whom The ancient Roman honour more appears Than any that draws breath in Italy.	**BASSANIO** Yes, my dearest friend, the kindest man, With the most willing heart and never tiring Of treating others with courtesy; and he's a man in whom The ancient Roman honour is more apparent Than in any other person throughout all Italy.
PORTIA What sum owes he the Jew?	**PORTIA** How much money does he owe the Jew?
BASSANIO For me three thousand ducats.	**BASSANIO** Three thousand ducats.
PORTIA What, no more? Pay him six thousand, and deface the bond; Double six thousand, and then treble that, Before a friend of this description Shall lose a hair through Bassanio's fault. First go with me to church and call me wife, And then away to Venice to your friend; For never shall you lie by Portia's side With an unquiet soul. You shall have gold To pay the petty debt twenty times over: When it is paid, bring your true friend along. My maid Nerissa and myself meantime Will live as maids and widows. Come, away! For you shall hence upon your wedding-day: Bid your friends welcome, show a merry cheer: Since you are dear bought, I will love you dear. But let me hear the letter of your friend.	**PORTIA** What! Is that all? Pay him six thousand and cancel the contract; I will pay double six thousand and then treble that, Before a friend like this Loses even one hair because of you, Bassanio. First go with me to the church and make me your wife, And then go to Venice to see your friend; Because I never want you to sleep next to me With an unsettled soul. I shall give you enough gold To pay this little debt twenty times over. When it is paid, bring your true friend back with you. In the meantime, my maid Nerissa and I Shall live as virgins and widows. Come on, let's go; Because you have to go away on your wedding day. Welcome your friends, put on a happy face; Since it's costing me dearly to marry you, I will love you dearly. But let me hear the letter from your friend.
BASSANIO [Reads] Sweet Bassanio, my ships have all miscarried, my creditors grow cruel, my estate is	**BASSANIO** 'Dear Bassanio, my ships have all sunk, my creditors are becoming mean, my financial state is very bad,

very low, my bond to the Jew is forfeit; and since in paying it, it is impossible I should live, all debts are cleared between you and I, if I might but see you at my death. Notwithstanding, use your pleasure: if your love do not persuade you to come, let not my letter. **PORTIA** O love, dispatch all business, and be gone! **BASSANIO** Since I have your good leave to go away, I will make haste: but, till I come again, No bed shall e'er be guilty of my stay, No rest be interposer 'twixt us twain. *Exeunt*	my contract with the Jew has to be honoured; and since, when I pay it, it will be impossible for me to live, all debts between us are cleared, if I can just see you before my death. Anyway, do what you think is best; if your love for me doesn't convince you to come, then don't let my letter persuade you.' **PORTIA** Oh my love, get organised and go! **BASSANIO** Since I am going with your blessing, I will go quickly; but, until I return, I won't go to bed, Nor sleep until I see you again. *Exeunt*

Translation of Act 3 Scene 3

ORIGINAL TEXT	MODERN TRANSLATION
Venice. A street.	**Venice. A street.**
Enter SHYLOCK, SALARINO, ANTONIO, and Gaoler	*Enter SHYLOCK, SALARINO, ANTONIO, and Gaoler*
SHYLOCK Gaoler, look to him: tell not me of mercy; This is the fool that lent out money gratis: Gaoler, look to him.	**SHYLOCK** Jailer, keep an eye on him. Don't talk to me about mercy – This is the fool who lent money without charging interest. Jailer, keep an eye on him.
ANTONIO Hear me yet, good Shylock.	**ANTONIO** Listen to what I have to say, good Shylock.
SHYLOCK I'll have my bond; speak not against my bond: I have sworn an oath that I will have my bond. Thou call'dst me dog before thou hadst a cause; But, since I am a dog, beware my fangs: The duke shall grant me justice. I do wonder, Thou naughty gaoler, that thou art so fond To come abroad with him at his request.	**SHYLOCK** I will have my bond; don't try to talk me out of taking my bond. I have sworn an oath which entitles me to have my bond. You called me a dog when you had no reason to, But, since I am a dog, beware of my fangs; The Duke will grant me justice. I am wondering, Jailer, why you're so agreeable To let him out at his request.
ANTONIO I pray thee, hear me speak.	**ANTONIO** Please, listen to what I have to say.
SHYLOCK I'll have my bond; I will not hear thee speak: I'll have my bond; and therefore speak no more. I'll not be made a soft and dull-eyed fool, To shake the head, relent, and sigh, and yield To Christian intercessors. Follow not; I'll have no speaking: I will have my bond.	**SHYLOCK** I will have my bond. I will not listen to you; I will have my bond; so don't say another thing. I will not be made a fool of, And shake my head, sigh and give in, To Christian appeals. Don't answer me; I don't want to hear anything; I want my bond.
Exit	*Exit*
SALARINO It is the most impenetrable cur That ever kept with men.	**SOLANIO** He is the most stubborn dog Who ever lived with humans.
ANTONIO Let him alone: I'll follow him no more with bootless prayers. He seeks my life; his reason well I know: I oft deliver'd from his forfeitures Many that have at times made moan to me; Therefore he hates me.	**ANTONIO** Leave him alone; I won't follow him around any more with futile pleas. He wants me dead; I'm well aware of the reason: I often paid off debts For many people who complained that they were unable to do so; So he hates me.

SALARINO I am sure the duke Will never grant this forfeiture to hold. **ANTONIO** The duke cannot deny the course of law: For the commodity that strangers have With us in Venice, if it be denied, Will much impeach the justice of his state; Since that the trade and profit of the city Consisteth of all nations. Therefore, go: These griefs and losses have so bated me, That I shall hardly spare a pound of flesh To-morrow to my bloody creditor. Well, gaoler, on. Pray God, Bassanio come To see me pay his debt, and then I care not! *Exeunt*	**SOLANIO** I am sure the Duke Will never permit this debt to be paid. **ANTONIO** The Duke can't prevent the law from taking its course; Because of the trade that foreign merchants do With us in Venice, if the law is disregarded, It will really call into question the integrity of the government, Since the trade and profit of our city Depends on many different nations. Therefore go; All this grief and loss has drained me so much That I'll hardly have a pound of flesh to spare To pay my bloody creditor tomorrow. Well jailer, onwards; Please God let Bassanio come To see me pay his debt and then I won't care about anything else. *Exeunt*

Translation of Act 3 Scene 4

ORIGINAL TEXT	MODERN TRANSLATION
Belmont. A room in PORTIA'S house.	**Belmont. A room in PORTIA'S house.**
Enter PORTIA, NERISSA, LORENZO, JESSICA, and BALTHASAR	*Enter PORTIA, NERISSA, LORENZO, JESSICA, and BALTHASAR*
LORENZO Madam, although I speak it in your presence, You have a noble and a true conceit Of godlike amity; which appears most strongly In bearing thus the absence of your lord. But if you knew to whom you show this honour, How true a gentleman you send relief, How dear a lover of my lord your husband, I know you would be prouder of the work Than customary bounty can enforce you.	**LORENZO** Madam, although I'm saying it directly to you, You have a really noble, genuine respect Of godlike friendship, which is very clear to see In how you're coping with the absence of your lord. But if you knew the man to whom you're showing this privilege, How much of a real gentleman you're helping, How dearly he loves your husband, I know you would be even prouder of what you're doing Than you would normally be.
PORTIA I never did repent for doing good, Nor shall not now: for in companions That do converse and waste the time together, Whose souls do bear an equal yoke Of love, There must be needs a like proportion Of lineaments, of manners and of spirit; Which makes me think that this Antonio, Being the bosom lover of my lord, Must needs be like my lord. If it be so, How little is the cost I have bestow'd In purchasing the semblance of my soul From out the state of hellish misery! This comes too near the praising of myself; Therefore no more of it: hear other things. Lorenzo, I commit into your hands The husbandry and manage of my house Until my lord's return: for mine own part, I have toward heaven breathed a secret vow To live in prayer and contemplation, Only attended by Nerissa here, Until her husband and my lord's return: There is a monastery two miles off; And there will we abide. I do desire you Not to deny this imposition; The which my love and some necessity Now lays upon you.	**PORTIA** I have never regretted doing good, And I won't now; because friends Who talk and spend a lot of time together, Who love each other equally, Must have a certain amount Of similarities regarding manners and spirit, Which makes me think that this Antonio, Being a bosom pal of my husband, Must inevitably be like my husband. If this is the case, How small the amount of money is that I'm providing To purchase freedom for someone who resembles Bassanio's very soul From a fate worse than death! It's starting to sound as if I'm praising myself; So, no more talk of that; I'll talk about other things. Lorenzo, I'm giving you the responsibility For the management and running of my house Until my husband's return; as for me, I have prayed a secret vow to God To live in prayer and contemplation, With only Nerissa's company, Until our husband's return. There is a monastery two miles away, And we will stay there. I really hope that You won't refuse this urgent request, Because I really need your help.

LORENZO Madam, with all my heart; I shall obey you in all fair commands.	**LORENZO** Madam, with all my heart I will do everything you ask of me.
PORTIA My people do already know my mind, And will acknowledge you and Jessica In place of Lord Bassanio and myself. And so farewell, till we shall meet again.	**PORTIA** My staff already know my wishes, And will accept you and Jessica as master and mistress of the house In place of Lord Bassanio and myself. So goodbye until we meet again.
LORENZO Fair thoughts and happy hours attend on you!	**LORENZO** May peace of mind and happy hours await you!
JESSICA I wish your ladyship all heart's content.	**JESSICA** I wish your ladyship your heart's desire.
PORTIA I thank you for your wish, and am well pleased To wish it back on you: fare you well Jessica.	**PORTIA** Thank you for your good wishes, and I'm very happy To wish you the same. Goodbye, Jessica.
Exeunt JESSICA and LORENZO	*Exit JESSICA and LORENZO*
Now, Balthasar, As I have ever found thee honest-true, So let me find thee still. Take this same letter, And use thou all the endeavour of a man In speed to Padua: see thou render this Into my cousin's hand, Doctor Bellario; And, look, what notes and garments he doth give thee, Bring them, I pray thee, with imagined speed Unto the tranect, to the common ferry Which trades to Venice. Waste no time in words, But get thee gone: I shall be there before thee.	Now, Balthasar, I have always found you to be honest and loyal, And I trust that you still are. Take this letter, And run as fast as you can To Padua; ensure that you put this letter Into my cousin's hands, Doctor Bellario; And take whatever papers and clothing he gives you, And bring them, please, as quickly as possible To the harbour, to the public ferry Which travels to and from Venice. Don't waste time talking, But get going; I'll be there before you.
BALTHASAR Madam, I go with all convenient speed.	**BALTHASAR** Madam, I'll go as fast as I can.
Exit	*Exit*
PORTIA Come on, Nerissa; I have work in hand That you yet know not of: we'll see our husbands Before they think of us.	**PORTIA** Come on, Nerissa, I have work to do That you know nothing about yet; we'll see our husbands Before they have a chance to think about us.
NERISSA Shall they see us?	**NERISSA** Will they see us?
PORTIA They shall, Nerissa; but in such a habit, That they shall think we are accomplished With that we lack. I'll hold thee any wager, When we are both accoutred like young men, I'll prove the prettier fellow of the two,	**PORTIA** They shall, Nerissa; but dressed in such a way That they'll think we're equipped With what we lack. I'll bet you anything, When we're both dressed like young men, I'll be the better looking of the two of us,

And wear my dagger with the braver grace, And speak between the change of man and boy With a reed voice, and turn two mincing steps Into a manly stride, and speak of frays Like a fine bragging youth, and tell quaint lies, How honourable ladies sought my love, Which I denying, they fell sick and died; I could not do withal; then I'll repent, And wish for all that, that I had not killed them; And twenty of these puny lies I'll tell, That men shall swear I have discontinued school Above a twelvemonth. I have within my mind A thousand raw tricks of these bragging Jacks, Which I will practise. **NERISSA** Why, shall we turn to men? **PORTIA** Fie, what a question's that, If thou wert near a lewd interpreter! But come, I'll tell thee all my whole device When I am in my coach, which stays for us At the park gate; and therefore haste away, For we must measure twenty miles to-day. *Exeunt*	And wear my dagger more dashingly, And speak like a teenage youth With a breaking voice; and change my feminine way of walking Into a manly stride; and talk about fights Like a bragging youth; and tell quirky lies, About how honourable ladies chased me, And then fell ill and died when I rejected them – I couldn't do anything about it. Then I'll repent, And wish, for all the world, that I had not killed them. And I'll tell twenty of these little lies, So that men will be convinced that I left school More than a year ago. I have in mind A thousand silly tricks like this, Which I'll use. **NERISSA** Why, are we going to turn into men? **PORTIA** For goodness sake, what sort of a question is that, If you had a dirty mind! But come here, I'll tell you my whole plan When I'm in my carriage, which is waiting for us At the park gate; so let's hurry up, Because we have twenty miles to travel today. *Exeunt*

Translation of Act 3 Scene 5

ORIGINAL TEXT	MODERN TRANSLATION
The same. A garden.	**The same. A garden.**
Enter LAUNCELOT and JESSICA	*Enter LAUNCELOT and JESSICA*
LAUNCELOT Yes, truly; for, look you, the sins of the father are to be laid upon the children: therefore, I promise ye, I fear you. I was always plain with you, and so now I speak my agitation of the matter: therefore be of good cheer, for truly I think you are damned. There is but one hope in it that can do you any good; and that is but a kind of bastard hope neither.	**LAUNCELOT** Yes, really; it's true that the sins of the father are passed down to their children; therefore , I promise you, I'm afraid for you. I've always been honest with you, so now I'm expressing my concerns; so cheer up, because I really think you're going to hell. There's only one hope for you that things will turn out well for you, and even that's a sort of illegitimate hope.
JESSICA And what hope is that, I pray thee?	**JESSICA** And what hope is that, please?
LAUNCELOT Marry, you may partly hope that your father got you not, that you are not the Jew's daughter.	**LAUNCELOT** You could hope that your father is not your biological father – that you are not the Jew's daughter.
JESSICA That were a kind of bastard hope, indeed: so the sins of my mother should be visited upon me.	**JESSICA** That really is a sort of illegitimate hope indeed; so the sins of my mother would then be passed down to me.
LAUNCELOT Truly then I fear you are damned both by father and mother: thus when I shun Scylla, your father, I fall into Charybdis, your mother: well, you are gone both ways.	**LAUNCELOT** Well then, I'm afraid you're cursed by both your father and your mother; so when I avoid Scylla, your father, I bump into Charybdis, your mother; well, you are doomed both ways.
JESSICA I shall be saved by my husband; he hath made me a Christian.	**JESSICA** I will be saved by my husband; he's made me a Christian.
LAUNCELOT Truly, the more to blame he: we were Christians enow before; e'en as many as could well live, one by another. This making Christians will raise the price of hogs: if we grow all to be pork-eaters, we shall not shortly have a rasher on the coals for money.	**LAUNCELOT** Really, more fool he; there were enough of us Christians before, as many as can comfortably live together. Making more people Christians will raise the price of pork; if we all turn into pork eaters, it won't be long before we won't be able to buy a rasher of bacon.
Enter LORENZO	*ENTER LORENZO*
JESSICA I'll tell my husband, Launcelot, what you say: here he comes.	**JESSICA** I'll tell my husband what you said, Launcelot. Here he comes.

LORENZO I shall grow jealous of you shortly, Launcelot, if you thus get my wife into corners.	**LORENZO** I'll be getting jealous of you in a minute Launcelot, if you keep taking my wife into corners like this.
JESSICA Nay, you need not fear us, Lorenzo: Launcelot and I are out. He tells me flatly, there is no mercy for me in heaven, because I am a Jew's daughter: and he says, you are no good member of the commonwealth, for in converting Jews to Christians, you raise the price of pork.	**JESSICA** No, you needn't worry about us, Lorenzo; Launcelot and I have fallen out; He tells me flatly that I won't go to heaven, because I'm a Jew's daughter; and he says that you're not a good member of the commonwealth, because, by converting Jews to Christians, you're raising the price of pork.
LORENZO I shall answer that better to the commonwealth than you can the getting up of the negro's belly: the Moor is with child by you, Launcelot.	**LORENZO** I can justify that better to the commonwealth than you can justify the swelling of the negro's belly; the Moor is pregnant by you, Launcelot.
LAUNCELOT It is much that the Moor should be more than reason: but if she be less than an honest woman, she is indeed more than I took her for.	**LAUNCELOT** It's too bad that there's more of the Moor than necessary; but if she's a less than honest woman, she's still more than I took her for.
LORENZO How every fool can play upon the word! I think the best grace of wit will shortly turn into silence, and discourse grow commendable in none only but parrots. Go in, sirrah; bid them prepare for dinner.	**LORENZO** Any fool can play with words! I think that soon silence will become the sure sign of wit, and talking will become desirable only in parrots. Go in and ask them to get ready for dinner.
LAUNCELOT That is done, sir; they have all stomachs.	**LAUNCELOT** That's been done, sir; they're ready to eat.
LORENZO Goodly Lord, what a wit-snapper are you! then bid them prepare dinner.	**LORENZO** Good Lord, what a wit you are! Then ask them to prepare dinner.
LAUNCELOT That is done too, sir; only 'cover' is the word.	**LAUNCELOT** That's been done too, sir, only ' lay the table' is what you need to say.
LORENZO Will you cover then, sir?	**LORENZO** Will you lay the table, then sir?
LAUNCELOT Not so, sir, neither; I know my duty.	**LAUNCELOT** No, I can't do that either, sir; I know my duty.
LORENZO Yet more quarrelling with occasion! Wilt thou show the whole wealth of thy wit in an instant? I pray tree, understand a plain man in his plain meaning: go to thy fellows; bid them cover the table, serve in the meat, and we will come in to dinner.	**LORENZO** Yet more mocking behaviour! Have you decided to display all of your wit at once? Please understand the straightforward meaning of what a straightforward man is trying to say: go to the servants, ask them to lay the table, bring in the meat, and we'll come to dinner.

<table>
<tr><td>LAUNCELOT
For the table, sir, it shall be served in; for the meat, sir, it shall be covered; for your coming in to dinner, sir, why, let it be as humours and conceits shall govern.

Exit</td><td>LAUNCELOT
As for the table, sir, dinner will be served on it; as for the meat, sir, it will be in covered dishes; as for you coming into dinner, sir, well just come in when you feel ready.

Exit</td></tr>
<tr><td>LORENZO
O dear discretion, how his words are suited!
The fool hath planted in his memory
An army of good words; and I do know
A many fools, that stand in better place,
Garnish'd like him, that for a tricksy word
Defy the matter. How cheerest thou, Jessica?
And now, good sweet, say thy opinion,
How dost thou like the Lord Bassanio's wife?</td><td>LORENZO
Oh goodness, how his words suit him!
The fool has memorised
An army of good words; and I know
Many fools that have better positions than him,
Appearing like him, who with a witty phrase
Go off the subject at hand. How are you, Jessica?
And now sweetheart, tell me your opinion,
How do you like Lord Bassanio's wife?</td></tr>
<tr><td>JESSICA
Past all expressing. It is very meet
The Lord Bassanio live an upright life;
For, having such a blessing in his lady,
He finds the joys of heaven here on earth;
And if on earth he do not mean it, then
In reason he should never come to heaven
Why, if two gods should play some heavenly match
And on the wager lay two earthly women,
And Portia one, there must be something else

Pawn'd with the other, for the poor rude world

Hath not her fellow.</td><td>JESSICA
I can't put it into words. It's very right
That Lord Bassanio should live an upright life,
Because, having such a wife is a blessing,
Giving him the joys of heaven here on earth;
And if he doesn't deserve it here on earth,
That means that he won't ever go to heaven.
If two gods should place a heavenly bet,
And the stakes had to be two earthly women,
If Portia was one of the women, there would have to be something else
Offered for the other woman; because the poor ordinary world
Has no-one like her.</td></tr>
<tr><td>LORENZO
Even such a husband
Hast thou of me as she is for a wife.</td><td>LORENZO
And that's the sort of husband
That you have in me, the equivalent of what Portia is as a wife.</td></tr>
<tr><td>JESSICA
Nay, but ask my opinion too of that.</td><td>JESSICA
But ask me my opinion about that too.</td></tr>
<tr><td>LORENZO
I will anon: first, let us go to dinner.</td><td>LORENZO
I will soon; first let's go to dinner.</td></tr>
<tr><td>JESSICA
Nay, let me praise you while I have a stomach.</td><td>JESSICA
No, let me praise you while I'm in the mood.</td></tr>
<tr><td>LORENZO
No, pray thee, let it serve for table-talk;
' Then, howso'er thou speak'st, 'mong other things
I shall digest it.</td><td>LORENZO
No, please, let's talk about it over our meal;
Then whatever you say, along with everything else
I shall digest it.</td></tr>
<tr><td>JESSICA
Well, I'll set you forth.

Exeunt</td><td>JESSICA
Well, I'll serve you up on the table.

Exit</td></tr>
</table>

Translation of Act 4 Scene 1

ORIGINAL TEXT	MODERN TRANSLATION
Venice. A court of justice.	**Venice. A court of justice.**
Enter the DUKE, the Magnificoes, ANTONIO, BASSANIO, GRATIANO, SALARINO, and others	*Enter the DUKE, the Magnificoes, ANTONIO, BASSANIO, GRATIANO, SALARINO, and others*
DUKE What, is Antonio here?	**DUKE** What, is Antonio here?
ANTONIO Ready, so please your grace.	**ANTONIO** I'm ready, your Grace.
DUKE I am sorry for thee: thou art come to answer A stony adversary, an inhuman wretch uncapable of pity, void and empty From any dram of mercy.	**DUKE** I am sorry for you; you have come to face A hard as nails enemy, an inhuman wretch, Incapable of pity, and completely void Of even a drop of mercy.
ANTONIO I have heard Your grace hath ta'en great pains to qualify His rigorous course; but since he stands obdurate And that no lawful means can carry me Out of his envy's reach, I do oppose My patience to his fury, and am arm'd To suffer, with a quietness of spirit, The very tyranny and rage of his.	**ANTONIO** I have heard that Your Grace has gone to great pains to contest His determined course of action; but since he remains stubborn, And there's no legal way to remove me From his malicious intent, I will match My patience with his fury, and I am prepared To suffer with a quiet spirit The extreme cruelty and rage of his.
DUKE Go one, and call the Jew into the court.	**DUKE** One of you go and call the Jew into the court.
SALARINO He is ready at the door: he comes, my lord.	**SALARINO** He is ready at the door; he's coming, my lord.
Enter SHYLOCK	*Enter SHYLOCK*
DUKE Make room, and let him stand before our face. Shylock, the world thinks, and I think so too, That thou but lead'st this fashion of thy malice To the last hour of act; and then 'tis thought Thou'lt show thy mercy and remorse more strange Than is thy strange apparent cruelty; And where thou now exact'st the penalty, Which is a pound of this poor merchant's flesh, Thou wilt not only loose the forfeiture, But, touch'd with human gentleness and love, Forgive a moiety of the principal;	**DUKE** Make room and let him stand infront of us. Shylock, everybody else thinks, and I think too, That you're giving this appearance of malice Right up until the last minute of this case; and then, it's thought, That you'll show your mercy and pity, which will be even stranger Than the strange cruelty you're showing now; And whereas now you're here to enforce the penalty, Which is a pound of this poor merchant's flesh, You will not only waive the forfeit, But, touched with human gentleness and love, Forgive a portion of the principal that he owes you,

Glancing an eye of pity on his losses, That have of late so huddled on his back,	And regard with pity the losses, That have recently been such a heavy burden for him to bear –
Enow to press a royal merchant down And pluck commiseration of his state From brassy bosoms and rough hearts of flint, From stubborn Turks and Tartars, never train'd To offices of tender courtesy. We all expect a gentle answer, Jew.	Enough to crush a royal merchant, And draw sympathy for his position From brash hearts and hard hearts of stone, From stubborn Turks and Tartars, never trained To have any tender ways at all. We all expect a noble answer from you, Jew.
SHYLOCK I have possess'd your grace of what I purpose; And by our holy Sabbath have I sworn To have the due and forfeit of my bond:	**SHYLOCK** I have informed your Grace of what I intend to do, And by our holy Sabbath I have sworn To have what is due to me, the penalty according to my contract.
If you deny it, let the danger light Upon your charter and your city's freedom. You'll ask me, why I rather choose to have A weight of carrion flesh than to receive Three thousand ducats: I'll not answer that:	If you don't allow it, then danger will come upon Your charter and your city's freedom. You're going to ask me why I prefer to have A pound of decaying flesh than to receive Three thousand ducats. I'm not going to answer that,
But, say, it is my humour: is it answer'd?	But just say it's the mood I'm in – does that answer it?
What if my house be troubled with a rat And I be pleased to give ten thousand ducats To have it baned? What, are you answer'd yet?	What if my house was troubled with a rat, And I was happy to pay ten thousand ducats To have it exterminated? Does that answer your question?
Some men there are love not a gaping pig; Some, that are mad if they behold a cat; And others, when the bagpipe sings i' the nose, Cannot contain their urine: for affection,	There are some men who don't love roast pork; There are some who go nuts if they see a cat; And others, when the bagpipes start playing, Can't help peeing themselves; because preferences which are,
Mistress of passion, sways it to the mood Of what it likes or loathes. Now, for your answer: As there is no firm reason to be render'd, Why he cannot abide a gaping pig; Why he, a harmless necessary cat; Why he, a woollen bagpipe; but of force Must yield to such inevitable shame As to offend, himself being offended;	In charge of passion, decide whether something Is liked or loathed. Now, for your answer: Just as there's no clear reason to be given Why one man can't bear roast pork; Why another one can't bear a harmless, useful cat; Why one, when he hears a bagpipe, is forced To urinate, followed by inevitable shame, Offending others as a result of being offended himself;
So can I give no reason, nor I will not, More than a lodged hate and a certain loathing	So I can't give a reason and I won't give a reason, Other than a deep seated hatred and a definite loathing
I bear Antonio, that I follow thus A losing suit against him. Are you answer'd?	Of Antonio, why I'm pursuing this Unprofitable lawsuit against him. Is that answer enough?
BASSANIO This is no answer, thou unfeeling man, To excuse the current of thy cruelty.	**BASSANIO** That's no answer, you heartless man, To excuse the enormity of your cruelty.
SHYLOCK I am not bound to please thee with my answers.	**SHYLOCK** I'm not obliged to please you with my answers.
BASSANIO Do all men kill the things they do not love?	**BASSANIO** Do all men kill what they don't love?

SHYLOCK Hates any man the thing he would not kill?	**SHYLOCK** Does any man hate something and not want to kill it?
BASSANIO Every offence is not a hate at first.	**BASSANIO** You shouldn't resort to hatred, the first time you're offended
SHYLOCK What, wouldst thou have a serpent sting thee twice?	**SHYLOCK** What, would you allow a snake to bite you twice?
ANTONIO I pray you, think you question with the Jew: You may as well go stand upon the beach And bid the main flood bate his usual height; You may as well use question with the wolf Why he hath made the ewe bleat for the lamb; You may as well forbid the mountain pines To wag their high tops and to make no noise, When they are fretten with the gusts of heaven; You may as well do anything most hard, As seek to soften that--than which what's harder?-- His Jewish heart: therefore, I do beseech you, Make no more offers, use no farther means, But with all brief and plain conveniency Let me have judgment and the Jew his will.	**ANTONIO** Please, think before you argue with the Jew. You may as well go and stand on the beach And ask the tide, which is in full flood, to go out; You may as well ask the wolf, Why he made the ewe bleat for her dead lamb; You may as well tell the mountain pines not to Wave their tree tops and not to make a sound When stormy winds gust from the heavens; You may as well attempt the hardest thing imaginable Than try to soften the thing – which is harder than anything else? – His Jewish heart. So I beg you, Make no more offers, don't try any other ways to change his mind, But as soon as it is possible Let me face the verdict, and let the Jew have his way.
BASSANIO For thy three thousand ducats here is six.	**BASSANIO** Instead of your three thousand ducats, here are six thousand ducats
SHYLOCK What judgment shall I dread, doing Were in six parts and every part a ducat, I would not draw them; I would have my bond.	**SHYLOCK** If every ducat in six thousand ducats Were divided into six parts, and every part was a ducat, I still would not take it; I would choose my legal contract.
DUKE How shalt thou hope for mercy, rendering none?	**DUKE** How can you ever hope for mercy for yourself, when you never show mercy to others?
SHYLOCK What judgment shall I dread, doing no wrong? You have among you many a purchased slave, Which, like your asses and your dogs and mules, You use in abject and in slavish parts, Because you bought them: shall I say to you, Let them be free, marry them to your heirs? Why sweat they under burthens? let their beds	**SHYLOCK** What judgement should I be dreading, when I've done nothing wrong? Many of you have bought slaves, Which, like your asses and your dogs and your mules, You use for dreadful jobs, Because you bought them; should I say to you 'Let them go free, let them marry your children – Why are you working them so hard? – Let their beds

Be made as soft as yours and let their palates Be season'd with such viands? You will answer 'The slaves are ours:' so do I answer you: The pound of flesh, which I demand of him, Is dearly bought; 'tis mine and I will have it. If you deny me, fie upon your law! There is no force in the decrees of Venice. I stand for judgment: answer; shall I have it?	Be as soft as your beds, and let their taste buds Be treated to the same food as yours are? You would answer 'They're our slaves'. So, in a similar way, I'm answering you: The pound of flesh which I'm demanding of him Is bought at great cost, it's mine, and I'm going to have it. If you refuse me, then shame upon your law! There is no power in the law of Venice. I want justice; answer me; am I going to get it?
DUKE Upon my power I may dismiss this court, Unless Bellario, a learned doctor, Whom I have sent for to determine this, Come here to-day.	**DUKE** I have the authority to dismiss this court, Unless Bellario, a legal expert, For whom I've sent to help me settle this matter, Arrives today.
SALARINO My lord, here stays without A messenger with letters from the doctor, New come from Padua.	**SALARINO** My lord, waiting outside is A messenger with letters from Bellario, the legal expert , Recently arrived from Padua.
DUKE Bring us the letter; call the messenger.	**DUKE** Bring us the letters; call in the messenger.
BASSANIO Good cheer, Antonio! What, man, courage yet! The Jew shall have my flesh, blood, bones and all, Ere thou shalt lose for me one drop of blood.	**BASSANIO** Cheer up, Antonio! Take courage, man! The Jew will have my flesh, blood, bones and everything, Before I let you lose even a drop of blood for me.
ANTONIO I am a tainted wether of the flock, Meetest for death: the weakest kind of fruit Drops earliest to the ground; and so let me You cannot better be employ'd, Bassanio, Than to live still and write mine epitaph.	**ANTONIO** I am like a weak sheep in a flock, Which deserves to die; the weakest fruit Drops to the ground first, so let me drop. You couldn't do anything better, Bassanio, Than to keep on living and write my epitaph.
Enter NERISSA, dressed like a lawyer's clerk	*Enter NERISSA, dressed like a lawyer's clerk*
DUKE Came you from Padua, from Bellario?	**DUKE** Have you come from Padua, from Bellario?
NERISSA From both, my lord. Bellario greets your grace.	**NERISSA** From both, my lord. Bellario sends greetings to you, your Grace.
Presenting a letter	*Presenting a letter*
BASSANIO Why dost thou whet thy knife so earnestly?	**BASSANIO** Why are you sharpening your knife so earnestly?
SHYLOCK To cut the forfeiture from that bankrupt there.	**SHYLOCK** To cut my penalty from that bankrupt over there.

GRATIANO Not on thy sole, but on thy soul, harsh Jew, Thou makest thy knife keen; but no metal can, No, not the hangman's axe, bear half the keenness Of thy sharp envy. Can no prayers pierce thee?	**GRATIANO** Not on your sole, but on your soul, cruel Jew, Is where you're sharpening your knife; but no metal could, Not even the hangman's axe, be even half as sharp As your hatred. Can't any prayers get through to you?
SHYLOCK No, none that thou hast wit enough to make.	**SHYLOCK** No, none that you're clever enough to say.
GRATIANO O, be thou damn'd, inexecrable dog! And for thy life let justice be accused. Thou almost makest me waver in my faith To hold opinion with Pythagoras, That souls of animals infuse themselves Into the trunks of men: thy currish spirit Govern'd a wolf, who, hang'd for human slaughter, Even from the gallows did his fell soul fleet, And, whilst thou lay'st in thy unhallow'd dam, Infused itself in thee; for thy desires Are wolvish, bloody, starved and ravenous.	**GRATIANO** Oh, damn you, disgusting dog! It's not right that you're alive. You almost make question my Christian faith, Making me agree with Pythagoras That the souls of animals are reincarnated In the bodies of humans. Your vile dog spirit Used to live in a wolf who, hanged for slaughtering humans, As he hung on the gallows, experienced his cruel soul passing out of his body, And whilst you lay in your unholy mother's womb, Reincarnated itself in you; that's why your desires Are wolfish, bloody, starved and ravenous.
SHYLOCK Till thou canst rail the seal from off my bond, Thou but offend'st thy lungs to speak so loud: Repair thy wit, good youth, or it will fall To cureless ruin. I stand here for law.	**SHYLOCK** Unless you can rant the signature off my contract, You're just damaging your lungs by speaking so loudly; Get your wits about you, young man, or you will fall Apart. I stand here with the law on my side.
DUKE This letter from Bellario doth commend A young and learned doctor to our court. Where is he?	**DUKE** This letter from Bellario commends A young and well educated legal expert to our court. Where is he?
NERISSA He attendeth here hard by, To know your answer, whether you'll admit him.	**NERISSA** He's waiting nearby To hear your answer, whether you'll let him come in.
DUKE With all my heart. Some three or four of you Go give him courteous conduct to this place. Meantime the court shall hear Bellario's letter.	**DUKE** With all my heart. Three or four of you Go and give him a polite and respectful welcome to this place. In the meantime, I'll read Bellario's letter to the court.
Clerk [Reads] Your grace shall understand that at the receipt of your letter I am very sick: but in the instant that your messenger came, in loving visitation was with me a young doctor of Rome; his name is Balthasar. I acquainted him with the cause in controversy between	**CLERK READS** 'Your Grace, please understand that when I received your letter I was already very ill; but at the time your messenger arrived, a friend of mine was visiting, a young lawyer from Rome – his name is Balthazar. I informed him about the controversial case between the Jew and Antonio the merchant; we consulted

the Jew and Antonio the merchant: we turned o'er many books together: he is furnished with my opinion; which, bettered with his own learning, the greatness whereof I cannot enough commend, comes with him, at my importunity, to fill up your grace's request in my stead. I beseech you, let his lack of years be no impediment to let him lack a reverend estimation; for I never knew so young a body with so old a head. I leave him to your gracious acceptance, whose trial shall better publish his commendation.	many books together; I have given him my opinion which, enhanced with his own expert opinion – the value of which I cannot commend highly enough – comes with him at my urgent request to answer your Grace's need in my place. I beg that you don't allow his youth to prevent you from holding him in high esteem, because I've never known such an old head on young shoulders. I commend him to you highly, but his legal work will commend him even more highly.'
DUKE You hear the learn'd Bellario, what he writes: And here, I take it, is the doctor come.	**DUKE** You hear what the learned Bellario has written; And here, I take it, is the doctor of law arriving.
Enter PORTIA, dressed like a doctor of laws	*Enter PORTIA, dressed like a doctor of laws*
Give me your hand. Come you from old Bellario?	May I shake your hand; have you come from old Bellario?
PORTIA I did, my lord.	**PORTIA** I have, my lord.
DUKE You are welcome: take your place. Are you acquainted with the difference That holds this present question in the court?	**DUKE** You are welcome; take your seat. Are you aquainted with the case That is currently being held in this court?
PORTIA I am informed thoroughly of the cause. Which is the merchant here, and which the Jew?	**PORTIA** Yes, I have been thoroughly informed about the case. Which one is the merchant and which one is the Jew?
DUKE Antonio and old Shylock, both stand forth.	**DUKE** Antonio and old Shylock, both come forward.
PORTIA Is your name Shylock?	**PORTIA** Is your name Shylock?
SHYLOCK Shylock is my name.	**SHYLOCK** Shylock is my name.
PORTIA Of a strange nature is the suit you follow; Yet in such rule that the Venetian law Cannot impugn you as you do proceed. You stand within his danger, do you not?	**PORTIA** The court case you're pursuing is of a most unusual nature; Yet there is no rule in Venetian law That can call into question your right to proceed. You are in peril from this man aren't you?
ANTONIO Ay, so he says.	**ANTONIO** Yes, so he says.

PORTIA Do you confess the bond?	**PORTIA** Do you acknowledge the contract?
ANTONIO I do.	**ANTONIO** I do.
PORTIA Then must the Jew be merciful.	**PORTIA** Then the Jew must be merciful to you.
SHYLOCK On what compulsion must I? tell me that.	**SHYLOCK** What would make me want to do that? Tell me.
PORTIA The quality of mercy is not strain'd, It droppeth as the gentle rain from heaven Upon the place beneath: it is twice blest; It blesseth him that gives and him that takes:	**PORTIA** The quality of mercy is not a forced thing; It drops as gently as the rain drops from heaven Upon the ground. Mercy brings a double blessing: It blesses the one who shows mercy and the one who receives mercy.
'Tis mightiest in the mightiest: it becomes	It is most powerful in the most powerful people; it is more attractive
The throned monarch better than his crown; His sceptre shows the force of temporal power,	In a royal king than even his crown is; His sceptre demonstrates the extent of his earthly power,
The attribute to awe and majesty, Wherein doth sit the dread and fear of kings; But mercy is above this sceptred sway; It is enthroned in the hearts of kings, It is an attribute to God himself; And earthly power doth then show likest God's When mercy seasons justice. Therefore, Jew, Though justice be thy plea, consider this, That, in the course of justice, none of us Should see salvation: we do pray for mercy; And that same prayer doth teach us all to render	Inspiring awe and majesty, Which engenders the dread and fear of kings; But mercy exceeds the influence of the sceptre, It is enthroned in the hearts of kings, It is a quality of God himself; And a king's power resembles God's power the most When mercy accompanies justice. So, Jew, Although you're asking for justice, think about this – That if justice is the requirement, then none of us Would be saved by God; we ask God for mercy, And knowing that we pray for mercy for ourselves, it teaches us to extend
The deeds of mercy. I have spoke thus much To mitigate the justice of thy plea;	Mercy to others. I have said all this To try to reduce the severity of your demand for justice,
Which if thou follow, this strict court of Venice Must needs give sentence 'gainst the merchant there.	Which if you pursue, this strict court of Venice Will have to carry out the sentence against this merchant.
SHYLOCK My deeds upon my head! I crave the law, The penalty and forfeit of my bond.	**SHYLOCK** Upon my head be it! I am adamant about the law, The penalty and payment of my contract.
PORTIA Is he not able to discharge the money?	**PORTIA** Isn't he able to pay back the money?
BASSANIO Yes, here I tender it for him in the court; Yea, twice the sum: if that will not suffice, I will be bound to pay it ten times o'er, On forfeit of my hands, my head, my heart: If this will not suffice, it must appear That malice bears down truth. And I beseech you, Wrest once the law to your authority:	**BASSANIO** Yes; I'll pay it for him now, in the court; Yes, twice the amount; if that's not enough, I will sign a contract to pay ten times that amount With my hands, head and heart as security; If this is not enough, it appears That it is true that you're truly malicious. I beg you, Use your authority to twist the law, just this once;

To do a great right, do a little wrong, And curb this cruel devil of his will.	Do a great right thing, by doing a little wrong thing, And stop this cruel devil from having his way.
PORTIA It must not be; there is no power in Venice Can alter a decree established: 'Twill be recorded for a precedent, And many an error by the same example Will rush into the state: it cannot be.	**PORTIA** That won't be allowed to happen; there is no power in Venice That can alter an established law; It would set a precedent, And when that example was followed, many wrong legal decisions Would be made all over the city; it cannot be done.
SHYLOCK A Daniel come to judgment! yea, a Daniel! O wise young judge, how I do honour thee!	**SHYLOCK** A Daniel has come to make a judgement! Yes, a Daniel! Oh, how I honour you, wise young judge!
PORTIA I pray you, let me look upon the bond.	**PORTIA** Please, allow me to look at the contract.
SHYLOCK Here 'tis, most reverend doctor, here it is.	**SHYLOCK** Here it is, most reverend Doctor; here it is.
PORTIA Shylock, there's thrice thy money offer'd thee.	**PORTIA** Shylock, you're being offered three times the money you lent.
SHYLOCK An oath, an oath, I have an oath in heaven: Shall I lay perjury upon my soul? No, not for Venice.	**SHYLOCK** An oath, an oath! I made an oath before God. Should I burden my soul with a breach of oath? No, not for all of Venice.
PORTIA Why, this bond is forfeit; And lawfully by this the Jew may claim A pound of flesh, to be by him cut off Nearest the merchant's heart. Be merciful: Take thrice thy money; bid me tear the bond.	**PORTIA** Well, this bond has to be paid; And this Jew may lawfully claim A pound of flesh, to be cut off by him Near to the merchant's heart. Show mercy. Take three times your money; tell me to tear up the contract.
SHYLOCK When it is paid according to the tenor. It doth appear you are a worthy judge; You know the law, your exposition Hath been most sound: I charge you by the law, Whereof you are a well-deserving pillar, Proceed to judgment: by my soul I swear There is no power in the tongue of man To alter me: I stay here on my bond.	**SHYLOCK** I will let you tear it up when it has been paid according to the law. It appears that you're a respectable judge; You know the law; you set forth your explanation Most soundly; I request that you, according to the law, Of which you are a fine upstanding representative, Deliver your verdict. I swear, on my soul There's nothing that anyone can say To change my mind. I am standing by my contract.
ANTONIO Most heartily I do beseech the court To give the judgment.	**ANTONIO** With all my heart, I beg the court To give the verdict.

PORTIA Why then, thus it is: You must prepare your bosom for his knife.	**PORTIA** Well then, this is it: You must prepare your chest for Shylock's knife.
SHYLOCK O noble judge! O excellent young man!	**SHYLOCK** Oh noble judge! Oh excellent young man!
PORTIA For the intent and purpose of the law Hath full relation to the penalty, Which here appeareth due upon the bond.	**PORTIA** Because the intent and purpose of the law Fully supports the payment of this penalty, Which is stated on this contract.
SHYLOCK 'Tis very true: O wise and upright judge! How much more elder art thou than thy looks!	**SHYLOCK** This is very true. Oh wise and upright judge, You are much more mature than you appear!
PORTIA Therefore lay bare your bosom.	**PORTIA** So, bare your chest.
SHYLOCK Ay, his breast: So says the bond: doth it not, noble judge? 'Nearest his heart:' those are the very words.	**SHYLOCK** Yes, his chest – That's what the contract says; doesn't it, noble judge? 'Nearest his heart', those are the exact words.
PORTIA It is so. Are there balance here to weigh The flesh?	**PORTIA** That's correct. Are there scales here to weigh The flesh?
SHYLOCK I have them ready.	**SHYLOCK** I have them ready.
PORTIA Have by some surgeon, Shylock, on your charge, To stop his wounds, lest he do bleed to death.	**PORTIA** Pay for a surgeon, Shylock, to stand by, To dress his wounds, otherwise he'll bleed to death.
SHYLOCK Is it so nominated in the bond?	**SHYLOCK** Is this request documented in the contract?
PORTIA It is not so express'd: but what of that? 'Twere good you do so much for charity.	**PORTIA** It is not requested, but so what? It would be good for you to do it to be charitable.
SHYLOCK I cannot find it; 'tis not in the bond.	**SHYLOCK** I can't find it; it's not written in the contract.
PORTIA You, merchant, have you any thing to say?	**PORTIA** You, merchant, do you have anything to say?
ANTONIO But little: I am arm'd and well prepared. Give me your hand, Bassanio: fare you well! Grieve not that I am fallen to this for you; For herein Fortune shows herself more kind	**ANTONIO** Not very much: I am ready and waiting. Give me your hand, Bassanio; goodbye. Don't grieve that this has happened to me because of you, Because, through this, Lady Luck is showing me more kindness

Than is her custom: it is still her use To let the wretched man outlive his wealth, To view with hollow eye and wrinkled brow An age of poverty; from which lingering penance Of such misery doth she cut me off. Commend me to your honourable wife: Tell her the process of Antonio's end; Say how I loved you, speak me fair in death; And, when the tale is told, bid her be judge Whether Bassanio had not once a love. Repent but you that you shall lose your friend, And he repents not that he pays your debt; For if the Jew do cut but deep enough, I'll pay it presently with all my heart.	Than she usually does. Her usual way is To let the wretched man live on after his wealth is gone, To face, with hollow eyes and wrinkled skin, His old age spent in poverty; from that lingering punishment Of sheer misery, Lady Luck has spared me. Remember me to your honourable wife; Explain to her how I came to my life's end; Tell her that I loved you; speak well of me after I have gone; And when the story is told, ask her to judge Whether Bassanio was once loved. Be sorry only that you're going to lose your friend, And he is not sorry that he is paying your debt; Because if the Jew cuts deeply enough, I'll pay it instantly with all my heart.
BASSANIO Antonio, I am married to a wife Which is as dear to me as life itself; But life itself, my wife, and all the world, Are not with me esteem'd above thy life: I would lose all, ay, sacrifice them all Here to this devil, to deliver you.	**BASSANIO** Antonio, I am married to a woman Who is as dear to me as life itself; But life itself, my wife, and the whole world, Are not more valuable to me than your life is; I would willingly lose everything, yes sacrifice them all To this devil here, to save you.
PORTIA Your wife would give you little thanks for that, If she were by, to hear you make the offer.	**PORTIA** Your wife wouldn't thank you for saying that, If she was here and heard you making that offer.
GRATIANO I have a wife, whom, I protest, I love: I would she were in heaven, so she could Entreat some power to change this currish Jew.	**GRATIANO** I have a wife who I truly love; I wish she was in heaven, so that she could Earnestly request some power to change this worthless Jew.
NERISSA 'Tis well you offer it behind her back; The wish would make else an unquiet house.	**NERISSA** It's just as well that you're making that offer behind your wife's back; Otherwise, that wish would cause arguments in the home.
SHYLOCK These be the Christian husbands. I have a daughter; Would any of the stock of Barrabas Had been her husband rather than a Christian! *Aside* We trifle time: I pray thee, pursue sentence.	**SHYLOCK** These are Christian husbands! I have a daughter – I wish that any of Barabbas' descendants Had become her husband, rather than a Christian! – *Aside* We're wasting time; please pronounce the sentence.
PORTIA A pound of that same merchant's flesh is thine: The court awards it, and the law doth give it.	**PORTIA** A pound of that merchant's flesh is yours. The court awards it and the court permits it.

SHYLOCK Most rightful judge!	**SHYLOCK** Most righteous judge!
PORTIA And you must cut this flesh from off his breast: The law allows it, and the court awards it.	**PORTIA** And you have to cut this flesh from his chest. The law allows it and the court awards it.
SHYLOCK Most learned judge! A sentence! Come, prepare!	**SHYLOCK** Most knowledgeable judge! The sentence! Come on, get ready!
PORTIA Tarry a little; there is something else. This bond doth give thee here no jot of blood; The words expressly are 'a pound of flesh:' Take then thy bond, take thou thy pound of flesh; But, in the cutting it, if thou dost shed One drop of Christian blood, thy lands and goods Are, by the laws of Venice, confiscate Unto the state of Venice.	**PORTIA** Wait a moment; there is something else. This contract doesn't permit you even a drop of blood: The words specify 'a pound of flesh'. So take what is legally yours, you take your pound of flesh; But, when you're cutting it, if you shed One drop of Christian blood, your property and belongings Are, by Venetian law, to be confiscated And given to the state of Venice.
GRATIANO O upright judge! Mark, Jew: O learned judge!	**GRATIANO** Oh upright judge! Take note, Jew. Oh knowledgeable judge!
SHYLOCK Is that the law?	**SHYLOCK** Is that the law?
PORTIA Thyself shalt see the act: For, as thou urgest justice, be assured Thou shalt have justice, more than thou desirest.	**PORTIA** You will see for yourself; Because, as you requested justice, be assured You shall receive justice, even more than you would like.
GRATIANO O learned judge! Mark, Jew: a learned judge!	**GRATIANO** Oh, learned judge! Take note, Jew. A learned judge!
SHYLOCK I take this offer, then; pay the bond thrice And let the Christian go.	**SHYLOCK** I will accept this offer then: pay me three times the amount of the loan, And let the Christian go.
BASSANIO Here is the money.	**BASSANIO** Here is the money.
PORTIA Soft! The Jew shall have all justice; soft! no haste: He shall have nothing but the penalty.	**PORTIA** Wait a minute! The Jew shall have justice. Wait! Don't rush. He won't be getting anything except the penalty.
GRATIANO O Jew! an upright judge, a learned judge!	**GRATIANO** Oh Jew! Such an upright judge, such a learned judge!

PORTIA Therefore prepare thee to cut off the flesh. Shed thou no blood, nor cut thou less nor more But just a pound of flesh: if thou cut'st more Or less than a just pound, be it but so much As makes it light or heavy in the substance, Or the division of the twentieth part Of one poor scruple, nay, if the scale do turn But in the estimation of a hair, Thou diest and all thy goods are confiscate.	**PORTIA** So, prepare yourself to cut off the flesh. Don't shed any blood and don't cut any more or any less Than just a pound of flesh; if you take more Or less than exactly one pound – even if it's as much As would cause it to weigh lighter or heavier, By just a twentieth Of one little gram; no, if the scales move Even by a hair's breadth – You will die, and all your goods will be confiscated.
GRATIANO A second Daniel, a Daniel, Jew! Now, infidel, I have you on the hip.	**GRATIANO** A second Daniel, a Daniel, Jew! Now, pagan, I've got you where I want you.
PORTIA Why doth the Jew pause? take thy forfeiture.	**PORTIA** Why is the Jew waiting? Take your penalty.
SHYLOCK Give me my principal, and let me go.	**SHYLOCK** Give my original 3000 ducats and let me go.
BASSANIO I have it ready for thee; here it is.	**BASSANIO** I have it ready for you; here it is.
PORTIA He hath refused it in the open court: He shall have merely justice and his bond.	**PORTIA** He has refused it before the court; He will have only justice and his penalty.
GRATIANO A Daniel, still say I, a second Daniel! I thank thee, Jew, for teaching me that word.	**GRATIANO** A Daniel, I maintain, a second Daniel! Thank you, Jew, for teaching me that word.
SHYLOCK Shall I not have barely my principal?	**SHYLOCK** Won't I even get the three thousand ducats I loaned him back?
PORTIA Thou shalt have nothing but the forfeiture, To be so taken at thy peril, Jew.	**PORTIA** You can't have anything except the penalty To be taken at your peril, Jew.
SHYLOCK Why, then the devil give him good of it! I'll stay no longer question.	**SHYLOCK** Well then, let him have it! I'm not arguing any more.
PORTIA Tarry, Jew: The law hath yet another hold on you. It is enacted in the laws of Venice, If it be proved against an alien That by direct or indirect attempts He seek the life of any citizen, The party 'gainst the which he doth contrive Shall seize one half his goods; the other half Comes to the privy coffer of the state; And the offender's life lies in the mercy Of the duke only, 'gainst all other voice.	**PORTIA** Wait, Jew. The law has yet another hold on you. It is stated in the laws of Venice that, If it is proved that a foreign resident Directly or indirectly attempts To kill any citizen, The person whom he was trying to kill Will take one half of his belongings; the other half Goes into the treasury of the state; And the offender's fate is in the hands Of only the Duke and no-one else.

In which predicament, I say, thou stand'st; For it appears, by manifest proceeding, That indirectly and directly too Thou hast contrived against the very life Of the defendant; and thou hast incurr'd The danger formerly by me rehearsed. Down therefore and beg mercy of the duke.	It is in this predicament that you find yourself; Because it is clearly evident That indirectly and directly too, You have contrived to take the life Of the defendant; and you have brought on yourself The peril that I have just recounted to you. So, down on your knees and beg the Duke for mercy.
GRATIANO Beg that thou mayst have leave to hang thyself: And yet, thy wealth being forfeit to the state, Thou hast not left the value of a cord; Therefore thou must be hang'd at the state's charge.	**GRATIANO** Beg that you'll be allowed to hang yourself; But since your wealth's being handed over to the state, You don't have sufficient money left to buy a rope; Therefore you must be hanged at the state's expense.
DUKE That thou shalt see the difference of our spirits, I pardon thee thy life before thou ask it: For half thy wealth, it is Antonio's; The other half comes to the general state, Which humbleness may drive unto a fine.	**DUKE** So that you can see the difference between our spirits, I am pardoning you from the death sentence before you even ask to be pardoned. Because half of your wealth goes to Antonio; The other half comes to the general state, Which, if you show humility, may be reduced to a fine.
PORTIA Ay, for the state, not for Antonio.	**PORTIA** Yes, the state's half may be reduced to fine; but not Antonio's half.
SHYLOCK Nay, take my life and all; pardon not that: You take my house when you do take the prop That doth sustain my house; you take my life When you do take the means whereby I live.	**SHYLOCK** No, take my life as well, don't grant me a pardon from death. You're taking my house when you take the support That keeps my house going; you're taking my life When you take away my means of making a living.
PORTIA What mercy can you render him, Antonio?	**PORTIA** What mercy can you offer him Antonio?
GRATIANO A halter gratis; nothing else, for God's sake.	**GRATIANO** A free rope; nothing else, for God's sake!
ANTONIO So please my lord the duke and all the court To quit the fine for one half of his goods, I am content; so he will let me have The other half in use, to render it, Upon his death, unto the gentleman That lately stole his daughter: Two things provided more, that, for this favour, He presently become a Christian; The other, that he do record a gift, Here in the court, of all he dies possess'd,	**ANTONIO** If my lord the Duke and all the court agree To let him off the fine for one half of his property; I am content, if he will let me have The other half in trust, to pass it over Upon his death, to the gentleman Who recently ran off with his daughter – Provided that he does two more things: That, in return for this favour, Shylock now becomes a Christian; The other thing, is that he makes a will, Here in this court, that when he dies all of his possessions,

Unto his son Lorenzo and his daughter.	Go to his son-in-law, Lorenzo, and his daughter.
DUKE He shall do this, or else I do recant The pardon that I late pronounced here.	**DUKE** He must do this, or else I will withdraw The pardon that I recently pronounced here.
PORTIA Art thou contented, Jew? what dost thou say?	**PORTIA** Are you satisfied, Jew? What do you say?
SHYLOCK I am content.	**SHYLOCK** I am satisfied.
PORTIA Clerk, draw a deed of gift.	**PORTIA** Clerk, draw up a document to make this official.
SHYLOCK I pray you, give me leave to go from hence; I am not well: send the deed after me, And I will sign it.	**SHYLOCK** Please, give me permission to leave here; I am not well; send the document after me And I will sign it.
DUKE Get thee gone, but do it.	**DUKE** Go then, but make sure you do it.
GRATIANO In christening shalt thou have two god-fathers: Had I been judge, thou shouldst have had ten more, To bring thee to the gallows, not the font.	**GRATIANO** When you're baptised a Christian, you have two God fathers; If I were the judge, you would have ten more, To bring you to the gallows, not to the font.
Exit SHYLOCK	*EXIT SHYLOCK*
DUKE Sir, I entreat you home with me to dinner.	**DUKE** Sir, I would really like you to come home with me for dinner.
PORTIA I humbly do desire your grace of pardon: I must away this night toward Padua, And it is meet I presently set forth.	**PORTIA** I humbly ask your Grace to excuse me; I must set off tonight for Padua, And it's only right that I set off as soon as possible.
DUKE I am sorry that your leisure serves you not. Antonio, gratify this gentleman, For, in my mind, you are much bound to him.	**DUKE** I am sorry that your time restriction doesn't allow you to stay. Antonio, give this gentleman a gift, Because, in my opinion, you owe him an awful lot.
Exeunt Duke and his train	*Exeunt Duke and his train*
BASSANIO Most worthy gentleman, I and my friend Have by your wisdom been this day acquitted Of grievous penalties; in lieu whereof, Three thousand ducats, due unto the Jew, We freely cope your courteous pains withal.	**BASSANIO** Most worthy gentleman, my friend and I Have today, by your wisdom, been let off From paying dreadful penalties; instead of giving The three thousand ducats which were due to the Jew, We give them to you freely with gratitude for your kind efforts.

ANTONIO And stand indebted, over and above, In love and service to you evermore.	**ANTONIO** We are indebted to you, way beyond this gift, In love and service forever.
PORTIA He is well paid that is well satisfied; And I, delivering you, am satisfied And therein do account myself well paid: My mind was never yet more mercenary. I pray you, know me when we meet again: I wish you well, and so I take my leave.	**PORTIA** Someone who is well satisfied with an outcome has been well paid, And I, by saving you, am satisfied, And therefore consider myself well paid. My thoughts were never on the money. I hope that you recognise me when we meet again; I wish you well and now I have to leave.
BASSANIO Dear sir, of force I must attempt you further: Take some remembrance of us, as a tribute, Not as a fee: grant me two things, I pray you, Not to deny me, and to pardon me.	**BASSANIO** Dear sir, I feel compelled to urge you; To take from us a memento, as a symbol of our affection, Instead of a fee. Please, do me two favours, Don't say no, and forgive me for persisting.
PORTIA You press me far, and therefore I will yield. *To ANTONIO* Give me your gloves, I'll wear them for your sake; *To BASSANIO* And, for your love, I'll take this ring from you: Do not draw back your hand; I'll take no more; And you in love shall not deny me this.	**PORTIA** You are persistent and so I will give in. *To ANTONIO* Give me your gloves, I'll wear them to remember you. *To BASSANIO* And, as a token of your affection, I'll accept this ring from you. Don't pull your hand back: I won't take anything else, And you, because of your grateful affection, won't refuse me it.
BASSANIO This ring, good sir, alas, it is a trifle! I will not shame myself to give you this.	**BASSANIO** This ring, kind sir – unfortunately, it's of little value; I will not embarrass myself by giving you this.
PORTIA I will have nothing else but only this; And now methinks I have a mind to it.	**PORTIA** I don't want anything else, only this; And now, I think, I've set my heart on it.
BASSANIO There's more depends on this than on the value. The dearest ring in Venice will I give you, And find it out by proclamation: Only for this, I pray you, pardon me.	**BASSANIO** There's more depending on this ring than merely its monetary value. I will give you the most expensive ring in Venice, And I'll find it by making an official announcement; But, as for this ring, please, I can't let you have it.
PORTIA I see, sir, you are liberal in offers You taught me first to beg; and now methinks You teach me how a beggar should be answer'd.	**PORTIA** I see, sir, you make extravagant offers; First you taught me to beg, and now, I think, You're teaching me how a beggar should be answered.

BASSANIO Good sir, this ring was given me by my wife; And when she put it on, she made me vow That I should neither sell nor give nor lose it.	**BASSANIO** Good sir, this ring was given to me by my wife; And, when she put it on me, she made me vow That I won't sell it, give it away or lose it.
PORTIA That 'scuse serves many men to save their gifts. An if your wife be not a mad-woman, And know how well I have deserved the ring, She would not hold out enemy for ever, For giving it to me. Well, peace be with you!	**PORTIA** That's an excuse many men would use to keep their gifts for themselves. If your wife is not a mad woman, And knew how much I deserve this ring, She wouldn't stay angry forever At you for giving it to me. Well, peace be with you!
Exeunt Portia and Nerissa	*Exeunt Portia and Nerissa*
ANTONIO My Lord Bassanio, let him have the ring: Let his deservings and my love withal Be valued against your wife's commandment.	**ANTONIO** My Lord Bassanio, let him have the ring. Think about how much he deserves it, and along with my deep friendship, Weigh that against your wife's order.
BASSANIO Go, Gratiano, run and overtake him; Give him the ring, and bring him, if thou canst, Unto Antonio's house: away! make haste.	**BASSANIO** Go, Gratiano, run and catch up with him; Give him the ring, and bring him, if you can, To Antonio's house. Go quickly.
Exit Gratiano	EXIT GRATIANO
Come, you and I will thither presently; And in the morning early will we both Fly toward Belmont: come, Antonio.	Come on, you and I will go shortly; And early in the morning we will both Hurry to Belmont. Come on, Antonio.
Exeunt	*Exeunt*

Translation of Act 4 Scene 2

ORIGINAL TEXT	MODERN TRANSLATION
The same. A street.	**The same. A street.**
Enter PORTIA and NERISSA	*Enter PORTIA and NERISSA*
PORTIA Inquire the Jew's house out, give him this deed And let him sign it: we'll away to-night And be a day before our husbands home: This deed will be well welcome to Lorenzo.	**PORTIA** Ask where the Jew's house is, give him this deed, And let him sign it; we'll leave tonight, And be home a day ahead of our husbands. Lorenzo will be well happy with this deed.
Enter GRATIANO	*Enter GRATIANO*
GRATIANO Fair sir, you are well o'erta'en My Lord Bassanio upon more advice Hath sent you here this ring, and doth entreat Your company at dinner.	**GRATIANO** Kind sir, you're lucky that I caught up with you. My Lord Bassanio, after more discussion, Has sent you this ring, and requests Your company for dinner.
PORTIA That cannot be: His ring I do accept most thankfully: And so, I pray you, tell him: furthermore, I pray you, show my youth old Shylock's house.	**PORTIA** I can't come for dinner. I do accept his ring with great thanks, And please tell him so. Also, Please can you show this young man the way to old Shylock's house.
GRATIANO That will I do.	**GRATIANO** I will do that.
NERISSA Sir, I would speak with you.	**NERISSA** Sir, I would like to speak with you.
Aside to PORTIA	*Aside to PORTIA*
I'll see if I can get my husband's ring, Which I did make him swear to keep for ever.	I'll see if I can get my husband's ring, Which I made him swear to keep forever.
PORTIA [Aside to NERISSA] Thou mayst, I warrant. We shall have old swearing That they did give the rings away to men; But we'll outface them, and outswear them too.	**PORTIA** (aside to Nerissa) I guarantee, you can. We'll have them swearing That they gave the rings away to men; But we'll confront them and outswear them too.
Aloud	*Aloud*
Away! make haste: thou knowist where I will tarry.	Go on, hurry up, you know where I'll be waiting.
NERISSA Come, good sir, will you show me to this house?	**NERISSA** Come on, good sir, can you show me to Shylock's house?
Exeunt	*Exeunt*

Translation of Act 5 Scene 1

ORIGINAL TEXT	MODERN TRANSLATION
Belmont. Avenue to PORTIA'S house.	**Belmont. Avenue to PORTIA'S house.**
Enter LORENZO and JESSICA	*Enter LORENZO and JESSICA*
LORENZO The moon shines bright: in such a night as this, When the sweet wind did gently kiss the trees And they did make no noise, in such a night Troilus methinks mounted the Troyan walls And sigh'd his soul toward the Grecian tents, Where Cressid lay that night.	**LORENZO** The moon shines bright. On a night like this, When the sweet wind gently kissed the trees, And they didn't make a sound – on a night like this, I think Troilus sat on the top of the walls of Troy, And his soul sighed towards the Greek camp, Where Cressida lay that night.
JESSICA In such a night Did Thisbe fearfully o'ertrip the dew And saw the lion's shadow ere himself And ran dismay'd away.	**JESSICA** On a night like this Thisby was nervously skipping through the dew, And saw the shadow of a lion, And ran away terrified.
LORENZO In such a night Stood Dido with a willow in her hand Upon the wild sea banks and waft her love To come again to Carthage.	**LORENZO** On a night like this Dido stood with a willow branch in her hand On the wild sea shore, to convey her lover Back to Carthage again.
JESSICA In such a night Medea gather'd the enchanted herbs That did renew old AEson.	**JESSICA** On a night like this Medea gathered the enchanted herbs Which rejuvenated old Aeson.
LORENZO In such a night Did Jessica steal from the wealthy Jew And with an unthrift love did run from Venice As far as Belmont.	**LORENZO** On a night like this Jessica stole from the wealthy Jew, And with a spendthrift lover she ran away from Venice As far as Belmont.
JESSICA In such a night Did young Lorenzo swear he loved her well, Stealing her soul with many vows of faith And ne'er a true one.	**JESSICA** On a night like this, Young Lorenzo swore he loved her very much, Stealing her soul with many vows of faith, And not one of them was true.
LORENZO In such a night Did pretty Jessica, like a little shrew, Slander her love, and he forgave it her.	**LORENZO** On a night like this Pretty Jessica, like a little shrew, Slandered her lover, and he forgave her for it.
JESSICA I would out-night you, did no body come; But, hark, I hear the footing of a man.	**JESSICA** I would outdo you in this 'on a night like this' competition, if no body interrupted us; But listen, I hear a man's footsteps.

Enter STEPHANO	*Enter STEPHANO*
LORENZO Who comes so fast in silence of the night?	**LORENZO** Who's in such a hurry in the dead of night?
STEPHANO A friend.	**STEPHANO** A friend.
LORENZO A friend! what friend? your name, I pray you, friend?	**LORENZO** A friend! What friend? What's your name, please friend?
STEPHANO Stephano is my name; and I bring word My mistress will before the break of day Be here at Belmont; she doth stray about By holy crosses, where she kneels and prays For happy wedlock hours.	**STEPHANO** Stephano is my name, and I bring news that My mistress will, before sunrise Be arriving here at Belmont; she's been staying at The monastery, where she's been kneeling and praying For a happy marriage.
LORENZO Who comes with her?	**LORENZO** Who's coming with her?
STEPHANO None but a holy hermit and her maid. I pray you, is my master yet return'd?	**STEPHANO** No one except her maid and a monk. Please tell me, has my master returned yet?
LORENZO He is not, nor we have not heard from him. But go we in, I pray thee, Jessica, And ceremoniously let us prepare Some welcome for the mistress of the house.	**LORENZO** No, he hasn't and we haven't heard from him either. But let's go in, please, Jessica, And formally prepare A welcome home ceremony for the mistress of the house.
Enter LAUNCELOT	*Enter LAUNCELOT*
LAUNCELOT Sola, sola! wo ha, ho! sola, sola!	**LAUNCELOT** Hey, hey! Hey! Yoo hoo!
LORENZO Who calls?	**LORENZO** Who's that calling out?
LAUNCELOT Sola! did you see Master Lorenzo? Master Lorenzo, sola, sola!	**LAUNCELOT** Hey! Have you seen Master Lorenzo? Master Lorenzo! Hey, hey!
LORENZO Leave hollaing, man: here.	**LORENZO** Stop yelling, man. Here I am!
LAUNCELOT Sola! where? where?	**LAUNCELOT** Hey! Where, where?
LORENZO Here.	**LORENZO** Here!

LAUNCELOT Tell him there's a post come from my master, with his horn full of good news: my master will be here ere morning. *Exit* **LORENZO** Sweet soul, let's in, and there expect their coming. And yet no matter: why should we go in? My friend Stephano, signify, I pray you, Within the house, your mistress is at hand; And bring your music forth into the air. *Exit Stephano* How sweet the moonlight sleeps upon this bank! Here will we sit and let the sounds of music Creep in our ears: soft stillness and the night Become the touches of sweet harmony. Sit, Jessica. Look how the floor of heaven Is thick inlaid with patines of bright gold: There's not the smallest orb which thou behold'st But in his motion like an angel sings, Still quiring to the young-eyed cherubins; Such harmony is in immortal souls; But whilst this muddy vesture of decay Doth grossly close it in, we cannot hear it. *Enter Musicians* Come, ho! and wake Diana with a hymn! With sweetest touches pierce your mistress' ear, And draw her home with music. *Music* **JESSICA** I am never merry when I hear sweet music. **LORENZO** The reason is, your spirits are attentive: For do but note a wild and wanton herd, Or race of youthful and unhandled colts, Fetching mad bounds, bellowing and neighing loud, Which is the hot condition of their blood; If they but hear perchance a trumpet sound, Or any air of music touch their ears, You shall perceive them make a mutual stand, Their savage eyes turn'd to a modest gaze By the sweet power of music: therefore the poet	**LAUNCELOT** Tell him there's a message come from my master full of good news; my master will be here in the morning. *Exit* **LORENZO** Sweet lady, let's go indoors, and wait for their arrival. But I suppose it doesn't matter - why do we have to go indoors? My friend Stephano, please inform, The household staff, your mistress is soon to arrive; And bring your musicians outdoors. *EXIT Stephano* How lovely is the moonlight resting on this bank! We'll sit here and let the sound of the music Drift into our ears; the soft stillness of the night Complements the sweet harmonies. Sit down, Jessica. Look how the floor of heaven Is thickly decorated with small bowls of bright gold; There's not the smallest star which you can see That doesn't, in its movement, sing like an angel, Even singing in concert to the young cherubims; Our immortal souls have the same kind of harmony, But whilst our earthly, decaying bodies Still physically contain it, we cannot hear it. Enter Musicians Come here and wake the goddess Diana with a hymn; With the sweetest notes fill your mistress' ear, And bring her home with music. *Music* **JESSICA** Sweet music never makes me happy. **LORENZO** The reason is that your soul is listening to the music; If you watch a wild and wilful herd, Or a few young, unbroken colts, Galloping around madly, whinnying and neighing loudly, Which they do because it's in their blood – If they just happen to hear the sound of a trumpet, Or, if any other kind of music reaches their ears, You will notice that they all stop in their tracks, Their wild eyes change into a peaceful gaze Through the power of sweet music. That's why the poet

Did feign that Orpheus drew trees, stones and floods; Since nought so stockish, hard and full of rage,	Pretended that the musician Orpheus made trees, stones and rivers come to him; Because there's nothing that's too stupid, hard or full of rage,
But music for the time doth change his nature. The man that hath no music in himself, Nor is not moved with concord of sweet sounds, Is fit for treasons, stratagems and spoils; The motions of his spirit are dull as night And his affections dark as Erebus: Let no such man be trusted. Mark the music.	That can't be changed by music. The man that has no music in his soul, Or is not moved by the harmony of sweet sounds, Is only fit for betrayals, scheming and plunderings; The activity of his soul is as dull as night, And his affections as dark as the underworld. No man like that should be trusted. Pay attention to the music.
Enter PORTIA and NERISSA	*Enter PORTIA and NERISSA*
PORTIA That light we see is burning in my hall. How far that little candle throws his beams!	**PORTIA** The light that we can see is coming from my hall. Look how far the beams of light spread from that little candle!
So shines a good deed in a naughty world.	That's the way a good deed shines out in a bad world.
NERISSA When the moon shone, we did not see the candle.	**NERISSA** When the moon was shining, we didn't see the candlelight.
PORTIA So doth the greater glory dim the less: A substitute shines brightly as a king Unto the king be by, and then his state	**PORTIA** Greater lights always outshine the lesser lights: A substitute shines as brightly as a king Until a king comes along and then the substitute's importance
Empties itself, as doth an inland brook Into the main of waters. Music! hark!	Diminishes, like a little stream flowing Into a huge river. Oh music! Listen!
NERISSA It is your music, madam, of the house.	**NERISSA** It's your musicians, madam from the house.
PORTIA Nothing is good, I see, without respect:	**PORTIA** I realise that you can't say anything's good without considering carefully;
Methinks it sounds much sweeter than by day.	I think the music sounds much better than it does in the daytime.
NERISSA Silence bestows that virtue on it, madam.	**NERISSA** The silence of the night makes the music sound better, madam.
PORTIA The crow doth sing as sweetly as the lark, When neither is attended, and I think The nightingale, if she should sing by day, When every goose is cackling, would be thought	**PORTIA** The crow sings as sweetly as the lark When no-one's listening; and I think The nightingale, if she sang in the daytime, When every goose is honking, wouldn't be considered
No better a musician than the wren. How many things by season season'd are	Any more tuneful than the wren. How many things in life are changed by time and place
To their right praise and true perfection!	To their rightful praise and true perfection!

Peace, ho! the moon sleeps with Endymion And would not be awaked.	Quiet now! The moon is sleeping with Endymion, her lover, And doesn't want to be woken.
Music ceases	*Music stops*
LORENZO That is the voice, Or I am much deceived, of Portia.	**LORENZO** That is the voice, If I'm not mistaken, of Portia.
PORTIA He knows me as the blind man knows the cuckoo, By the bad voice.	**PORTIA** He recognises me like a blind man recognises the cuckoo, By the bad voice.
LORENZO Dear lady, welcome home.	**LORENZO** Dear lady, welcome home.
PORTIA We have been praying for our husbands' healths, Which speed, we hope, the better for our words. Are they return'd?	**PORTIA** We have been praying for our husbands' welfare, We hope that our words have been successful. Have they returned yet?
LORENZO Madam, they are not yet; But there is come a messenger before, To signify their coming.	**LORENZO** Madam, they're not here yet; But a messenger has been here, To inform us that they're on their way.
PORTIA Go in, Nerissa; Give order to my servants that they take No note at all of our being absent hence; Nor you, Lorenzo; Jessica, nor you.	**PORTIA** Go indoors, Nerissa; Order my servants that they make No mention at all of our absence from here; Nor you, Lorenzo; nor you, Jessica
A tucket sounds	*A tucket sounds*
LORENZO Your husband is at hand; I hear his trumpet: We are no tell-tales, madam; fear you not.	**LORENZO** Your husband is approaching; I can hear his trumpet. We are not tell-tales, madam, don't worry.
PORTIA This night methinks is but the daylight sick; It looks a little paler: 'tis a day, Such as the day is when the sun is hid.	**PORTIA** I think this night is just like sickly daylight; It only looks a bit paler; it's like a day The sort of day when the sun is hidden.
Enter BASSANIO, ANTONIO, GRATIANO, and their followers	*Enter BASSANIO, ANTONIO, GRATIANO, and their followers*
BASSANIO We should hold day with the Antipodes, If you would walk in absence of the sun.	**BASSANIO** We would have daylight equal to that on the opposite side of the world, If you walked outside at night.
PORTIA Let me give light, but let me not be light;	**PORTIA** Let me give light, but may I never be light, as in having loose morals,

For a light wife doth make a heavy husband, And never be Bassanio so for me: But God sort all! You are welcome home, my lord.	Because a light, loose moralled wife causes a heavy burden for her husband, And I never want Bassanio to be like that because of me; But God take care of everything! You are welcome home, my lord.
BASSANIO I thank you, madam. Give welcome to my friend. This is the man, this is Antonio, To whom I am so infinitely bound.	**BASSANIO** Thank you, madam; please welcome my friend. This is the man, this is Antonio, To whom I am forever indebted.
PORTIA You should in all sense be much bound to him. For, as I hear, he was much bound for you.	**PORTIA** You should in every sense of the word be indebted to him. Because I have heard that he was in a lot of debt for you.
ANTONIO No more than I am well acquitted of.	**ANTONIO** I have been released from all that debt.
PORTIA Sir, you are very welcome to our house: It must appear in other ways than words, Therefore I scant this breathing courtesy.	**PORTIA** Sir, you are very welcome to our home. Your welcome must be demonstrated by more than just words, So I'll cut short the niceties.
GRATIANO [To NERISSA] By yonder moon I swear you do me wrong; In faith, I gave it to the judge's clerk: Would he were gelt that had it, for my part, Since you do take it, love, so much at heart.	**GRATIANO TO NERISSA** I swear, by that moon over there, that you're wronging me; Truthfully, I gave it to the judge's clerk. I wish that he'd been castrated now, Since you've taken it to heart so much, my love.
PORTIA A quarrel, ho, already! what's the matter?	**PORTIA** What! An argument already! What's the matter?
GRATIANO About a hoop of gold, a paltry ring That she did give me, whose posy was For all the world like cutler's poetry Upon a knife, 'Love me, and leave me not.'	**GRATIANO** It's about a hoop of gold, an insignificant ring That she gave me, whose inscription was For all the world like a cutlery maker's poetry On a knife, 'Love me and don't leave me'.
NERISSA What talk you of the posy or the value? You swore to me, when I did give it you, That you would wear it till your hour of death And that it should lie with you in your grave: Though not for me, yet for your vehement oaths, You should have been respective and have kept it. Gave it a judge's clerk! no, God's my judge, The clerk will ne'er wear hair on's face that had it.	**NERISSA** Why are you talking about the quality of the inscription or the value of the ring? You swore to me, when I gave it to you, That you would wear it until you died, And that it would go with you to your grave; If not for my sake, then because of your earnest vows, You should have been respectful and kept it. You gave it to a judge's clerk! No, as God's my judge, The clerk you gave it to will never grow a beard.
GRATIANO He will, an if he live to be a man.	**GRATIANO** He will, if he lives long enough to become a man.

NERISSA Ay, if a woman live to be a man.	**NERISSA** Yes, if a woman lives long enough to become a man.
GRATIANO Now, by this hand, I gave it to a youth, A kind of boy, a little scrubbed boy, No higher than thyself; the judge's clerk, A prating boy, that begg'd it as a fee: I could not for my heart deny it him.	**GRATIANO** I swear that I gave it to a youth, A kind of boy, a fresh faced little boy No taller than you, the judges clerk; A talkative boy who wanted it as payment; I didn't have the heart to say no to him.
PORTIA You were to blame, I must be plain with you, To part so slightly with your wife's first gift: A thing stuck on with oaths upon your finger And so riveted with faith unto your flesh. I gave my love a ring and made him swear Never to part with it; and here he stands; I dare be sworn for him he would not leave it Nor pluck it from his finger, for the wealth That the world masters. Now, in faith, Gratiano, You give your wife too unkind a cause of grief: An 'twere to me, I should be mad at it.	**PORTIA** I must be honest with you, you were wrong, To part so easily with your wife's first gift, A thing placed, with vows, on your finger And firmly fixed, with faith, to your body. I gave my love a ring, and made him swear Never to part with it, and here he is; I would swear on his behalf, that he wouldn't leave it behind Or even take it off his finger for all the money In the world. Now, honestly, Gratiano, Your thoughtlessness has caused your wife's grief; And if it were me, I would be just as upset.
BASSANIO [Aside] Why, I were best to cut my left hand off And swear I lost the ring defending it.	**BASSANIO** (ASIDE) Perhaps I'd better cut my left hand off, And swear that I lost the ring defending it.
GRATIANO My Lord Bassanio gave his ring away Unto the judge that begg'd it and indeed Deserved it too; and then the boy, his clerk, That took some pains in writing, he begg'd mine; And neither man nor master would take aught But the two rings.	**GRATIANO** My Lord Bassanio gave his ring away To the judge who begged him for it, and indeed Deserved it too; and then the boy, his clerk, Who took great care with the documentation, he begged for my ring; And neither the man nor the master would take anything But the two rings.
PORTIA What ring gave you my lord? Not that, I hope, which you received of me.	**PORTIA** Which ring did you give away, my lord? Not the one, I hope, that I gave you.
BASSANIO If I could add a lie unto a fault, I would deny it; but you see my finger Hath not the ring upon it; it is gone.	**BASSANIO** If I could lie about my mistake, I would deny it; but you can see that my finger Doesn't have the ring on it; it is gone.
PORTIA Even so void is your false heart of truth. By heaven, I will ne'er come in your bed Until I see the ring.	**PORTIA** Just as your finger is void of the ring, likewise your false heart is void of the truth; I swear, I will never get into bed with you Until I see the ring.
NERISSA Nor I in yours Till I again see mine.	**NERISSA** Me neither, Gratiano Until I see my ring again.

BASSANIO Sweet Portia, If you did know to whom I gave the ring, If you did know for whom I gave the ring And would conceive for what I gave the ring And how unwillingly I left the ring, When nought would be accepted but the ring, You would abate the strength of your displeasure.	**BASSANIO** Sweet Portia, If you knew who I gave the ring to, If you knew for whose sake I gave him the ring, And could understand why I gave him the ring, And how unwillingly I was parted from the ring, When he wouldn't accept anything but the ring, You wouldn't be nearly as angry as you are now.
PORTIA If you had known the virtue of the ring, Or half her worthiness that gave the ring, Or your own honour to contain the ring, You would not then have parted with the ring. What man is there so much unreasonable, If you had pleased to have defended it With any terms of zeal, wanted the modesty To urge the thing held as a ceremony? Nerissa teaches me what to believe: I'll die for't but some woman had the ring.	**PORTIA** If you had known how very special the ring was, Or even half the worthiness of the woman who gave the ring to you, Or your own great self respect in keeping the ring, You would not have parted with the ring. What kind of man would be so unreasonable, If you had really tried to keep the ring With any determination, as to lack enough self restraint To pursue something that holds great ceremonial value? I agree with what Nerissa thinks: I'll swear on my life that you gave the ring to some woman.
BASSANIO No, by my honour, madam, by my soul, No woman had it, but a civil doctor, Which did refuse three thousand ducats of me And begg'd the ring; the which I did deny him And suffer'd him to go displeased away; Even he that did uphold the very life Of my dear friend. What should I say, sweet lady? I was enforced to send it after him; I was beset with shame and courtesy; My honour would not let ingratitude So much besmear it. Pardon me, good lady; For, by these blessed candles of the night, Had you been there, I think you would have begg'd The ring of me to give the worthy doctor.	**BASSANIO** No, on my honour, madam, I swear, I didn't give it to a woman, but to a civil lawyer, Who refused to accept three thousand ducats in payment from me, And begged, instead, for the ring; which I denied him, And caused him to leave disappointed- Even though he had saved the life Of my dear friend. What could I say, sweet lady? I felt obliged to send the ring after him; I was overcome with shame and respect; I couldn't let ingratitude cause my honour To be brought into disrepute. Forgive me, good lady; Because, by these holy candles of the night, If you'd been there, I think you would have begged Me to give my ring to the worthy lawyer.
PORTIA Let not that doctor e'er come near my house: Since he hath got the jewel that I loved, And that which you did swear to keep for me, I will become as liberal as you; I'll not deny him any thing I have, No, not my body nor my husband's bed: Know him I shall, I am well sure of it: Lie not a night from home; watch me like Argus: If you do not, if I be left alone, Now, by mine honour, which is yet mine own, I'll have that doctor for my bedfellow.	**PORTIA** Don't let that lawyer ever come near my house; Since he has the jewel that I loved, Which you swore to me to keep forever, I will become as liberal as you; I won't deny him anything I have, Not even my body nor my husband's bed. I'll recognise him, I can assure you of that. So don't spend a night away from home; Watch me like Argus and his hundred eyes; If you don't, if I'm left alone, I swear by my honour which is still my own, I'll have that lawyer as my bedfellow.

NERISSA And I his clerk; therefore be well advised How you do leave me to mine own protection.	**NERISSA** And I'll have his clerk; so be warned About leaving me on my own.
GRATIANO Well, do you so; let not me take him, then; For if I do, I'll mar the young clerk's pen.	**GRATIANO** Well, do as you wish, but don't let me catch him; Because if I do, I'll break that young clerk's pen.
ANTONIO I am the unhappy subject of these quarrels.	**ANTONIO** I am the unhappy subject of these quarrels.
PORTIA Sir, grieve not you; you are welcome notwithstanding.	**PORTIA** Sir, don't be sad; you're welcome here despite everything.
BASSANIO Portia, forgive me this enforced wrong; And, in the hearing of these many friends, I swear to thee, even by thine own fair eyes, Wherein I see myself--	**BASSANIO** Portia, forgive me for this unavoidable mistake; And in the hearing of these many friends I swear to you, by your own beautiful eyes, In which I see myself reflected
PORTIA Mark you but that! In both my eyes he doubly sees himself; In each eye, one: swear by your double self, And there's an oath of credit.	**PORTIA** Listen to that! He sees himself in both of my eyes, so there are two of him, One in each eye; swear by your double minded self, And that's an oath I can believe.
BASSANIO Nay, but hear me: Pardon this fault, and by my soul I swear I never more will break an oath with thee.	**BASSANIO** No, just hear what I want to say. Forgive this mistake, and I swear, by my soul That I'll never again break a promise to you.
ANTONIO I once did lend my body for his wealth; Which, but for him that had your husband's ring, Had quite miscarried: I dare be bound again, My soul upon the forfeit, that your lord Will never more break faith advisedly.	**ANTONIO** I once lent my body to prosper him, Which, if not for the lawyer who had your husband's ring, Would have gone very wrong; I would be guarantor again, And offer my soul as the forfeit, for your husband That he will never again knowingly break a promise.
PORTIA Then you shall be his surety. Give him this And bid him keep it better than the other.	**PORTIA** Then you can be his guarantor. Give him this, And ask him to look after it better than the other one.
ANTONIO Here, Lord Bassanio; swear to keep this ring.	**ANTONIO** Here, Lord Bassanio, swear that you'll keep this ring.
BASSANIO By heaven, it is the same I gave the doctor!	**BASSANIO** Heavens above, it's the same one I gave to the lawyer!
PORTIA I had it of him: pardon me, Bassanio;	**PORTIA** I got it from him. Forgive me, Bassanio,

For, by this ring, the doctor lay with me.	Because, for this ring, I slept with the lawyer.
NERISSA And pardon me, my gentle Gratiano; For that same scrubbed boy, the doctor's clerk, In lieu of this last night did lie with me.	**NERISSA** And forgive me, my gentle Gratiano, Because the fresh faced boy, the lawyer's clerk, Slept with me last night, in exchange for this ring.
GRATIANO Why, this is like the mending of highways In summer, where the ways are fair enough: What, are we cuckolds ere we have deserved it?	**GRATIANO** Well, this is like the repairing of roads In the summer, when the roads don't need to be repaired. What, have you been unfaithful to us before we've deserved it?
PORTIA Speak not so grossly. You are all amazed: Here is a letter; read it at your leisure; It comes from Padua, from Bellario: There you shall find that Portia was the doctor, Nerissa there her clerk: Lorenzo here Shall witness I set forth as soon as you And even but now return'd; I have not yet Enter'd my house. Antonio, you are welcome; And I have better news in store for you Than you expect: unseal this letter soon; There you shall find three of your argosies Are richly come to harbour suddenly: You shall not know by what strange accident I chanced on this letter.	**PORTIA** Don't speak so coarsely. You all look amazed. Here's a letter; read it at your leisure; It's come from Padua, from Bellario; You will find that Portia was the lawyer, Nerissa was her clerk. Lorenzo here Will confirm that I set out when you did, And have only just returned; I have not yet Even entered my house. Antonio, you are welcome; And I have better news waiting for you Than you expect. Open this letter soon; There you will discover that three of your ships Have suddenly sailed into harbour lsaden with riches. You'll never know by what strange coincidence it was I came across this letter.
ANTONIO I am dumb.	**ANTONIO** I am dumbstruck.
BASSANIO Were you the doctor and I knew you not?	**BASSANIO** Were you the lawyer and I didn't recognise you?
GRATIANO Were you the clerk that is to make me cuckold?	**GRATIANO** Were you the clerk that my wife is to be unfaithful with?
NERISSA Ay, but the clerk that never means to do it, Unless he live until he be a man.	**NERISSA** Yes, but the clerk will never do it, Unless he grows into a man.
BASSANIO Sweet doctor, you shall be my bed-fellow: When I am absent, then lie with my wife.	**BASSANIO** Sweet lawyer, you shall come to bed with me; When I'm away, then sleep with my wife.
ANTONIO Sweet lady, you have given me life and living; For here I read for certain that my ships Are safely come to road.	**ANTONIO** Sweet lady, you have given me life and a living too; Because I read here that my ships have definitely Come safely into harbour.
PORTIA How now, Lorenzo!	**PORTIA** How's it going, Lorenzo!

My clerk hath some good comforts too for you.	My clerk has some comforting news for you too.
NERISSA Ay, and I'll give them him without a fee. There do I give to you and Jessica, From the rich Jew, a special deed of gift, After his death, of all he dies possess'd of.	**NERISSA** Yes, and I'll give it to him free of charge. I give to you and Jessica, From the rich Jew, a special last will and testament, Of all that he possesses when he dies.
LORENZO Fair ladies, you drop manna in the way Of starved people.	**LORENZO** Beautiful ladies, you're dropping manna from heaven on starving people.
PORTIA It is almost morning, And yet I am sure you are not satisfied Of these events at full. Let us go in; And charge us there upon inter'gatories, And we will answer all things faithfully.	**PORTIA** It's almost morning, And yet I'm sure you're not satisfied Fully about what happened. Let's go indoors, And you can ask us all your questions there, And we will answer everything truthfully.
GRATIANO Let it be so: the first inter'gatory That my Nerissa shall be sworn on is, Whether till the next night she had rather stay, Or go to bed now, being two hours to day: But were the day come, I should wish it dark, That I were couching with the doctor's clerk. Well, while I live I'll fear no other thing So sore as keeping safe Nerissa's ring.	**GRATIANO** OK, then. The first question That my Nerissa will be asked is, Whether she'd rather stay awake until tomorrow night, Or go to bed now, even though it's only two hours until dawn. But when the day comes, I'll wish it was night time, So I could sleep with the lawyer's clerk. Well, as long as I live, I won't worry about anything More than keeping Nerissa's ring safe.
Exeunt	*Exit*

29654998R00070

Printed in Great Britain
by Amazon